Thriving Amidst Cancer: A General's Strategy to Find Hope While Fighting Prostate Cancer

Roger VanderKolk

Blauw Shack Media

Blauw Shack Media

ISBN: 979-8-9867313-0-8 (paperback)
ISBN: 979-8-9867313-1-5 (hard cover)

Cover Art by Kirstin Vincent

Dedicated to Brigadier General Bruce Wiley VanderKolk. Forever in our hearts. Forever a legacy in which for us to strive.

Foreword

Over the years as a minister I have met a lot of people. Some of those people stand out more than others. Some of them you say to yourself, "It was such a blessing to know that person." Bruce VanderKolk was one of those blessings. I had the privilege of serving under Bruce, alongside of Bruce, and simply walking with him as a friend. His son, Roger, has done a great job capturing Bruce's heart, life and faith. Bruce was a quiet man and somewhat private in his personal feelings, but what is shared in this book gives wisdom and insight that will be a blessing to many. As you read and reflect, may you be one of those who receive a blessing from his life.

Jeff Chitwood - Pastor, Anchor Christian Church, Bonita Springs, FL

Cancer

I Respect No One

"I respect no one.
Not the young nor the old.
Not the rich nor the poor.
Like a thief in the night,
I prey upon the unexpected.

I am silent,
    For awhile.
You do not hear me;
    You do not see me;
        You cannot sense me
I am there but not seen.

You cannot run,
    You cannot hide.
You may be strong,
    I am stronger.
You may be on top,
    I will bring you down.
The sun may shine,
    I will bring storms.

I invade your structure;
    Invisible.
I take over space,
    Multiplying.
I destroy as I go,
    Killing good;
    Spreading death.

On my terms I will
    Reveal myself.

(Spoken by Cancer)

Bruce W. VanderKolk (Oct 17, 2015)

Preface

Author's Right to Write

My right to write came through the cancer journey with my mother, my grandmother, a cousin, and my father Bruce. I can relate to what your family is going through because my family has gone through a similar journey. After studying Bruce's journal, I can empathize with your experience and pull tidbits from the multitude of his experiences with major illnesses to provide advice on how to have hope during the struggle.

Perhaps my defining characteristic of a right to write about Bruce's journey is that he was my father.

I can tell you story after story after story of personal observations of how Bruce did not let his struggles with cancer and other illnesses negatively affect his daily life. One example: In June of 2013, my parents drove from their home in northern Illinois to my house in Woodbury, a suburb of St. Paul, MN. As you'll later read, this was during the time when Bruce was 4 years free from the prostate cancer but he was still dealing with the various side effects from the removal of the prostate. In addition he was still dealing with issues from the hernia and thyroid surgeries. Despite all of his issues, we had a great weekend. We took a day and drove to Duluth and explored the famed North Shore. We visited Superior, WI, and made plans to come back and visit the Apostle Islands at a future time. He and Mom made a couple of trips to downtown Stillwater, MN, which was one of their favorite places. Dad and I went to the local shooting range. I even was able to convince them to attend a worship service at the church I was attending that was very contemporary (they preferred a traditional service with fewer guitars, no back-up singers, and absolutely no drum sets). It was a great weekend because Dad focused on others rather than himself.

There are many other examples as well such as the family trip we made to Disney in January of 2011, Easter in Minneapolis later in 2011, and many more.

Bruce was an expert on how to thrive during cancer, having battled one serious illness after another between the years of 2009 to 2017. Unfortunately he is no longer around to offer this advice to others engaged in similar struggles. That's why I'm sharing my exposition of his message with you.

Treatment of Bruce's Writings

In many respects this book was easy to write because the bulk of the text was pulled from various writings of Bruce's while he was fighting cancer and other diseases. But it was necessary to make some revisions to his writings in order to have the work published. The grammar was improved in certain areas to improve the presentation of his words, but the content and message behind the writings is unchanged.

To foster anonymity, the specific physician, medical facility, and friends that Bruce recorded in his journal have been removed from this book. The word "doctor" is used to disguise the specific medical practitioner and the word "medical facility" is used to disguise the specific medical practice that Bruce recorded in his journal.

Sometimes, Bruce gets very technical and detailed in his writings about the various conditions of the cancer or illness. For the most part, this information was included in the book because it might connect with people going through the same struggle and provide some level of comfort and/or encouragement.

All non-journal writings by Bruce during his struggle are referenced at the conclusion of the writing with his name and date of the writing.

The remainder of the book is written by the author. This includes the call-outs, the concept of thriving amidst the disease, and other content. The goal of this content is to peer into Bruce's life and project what he would want to convey.

Special treatment has been applied to the fonts of the two authors: Bruce's words will be treated in *Italics* format while the words of the author will be normal font.

The First in a Series

When this project was started, the initial plan was to transform Dad's journal into one book. However, the amount of content that was in his journals quickly led to the realization that two books would be necessary to adequately deliver Dad's message. A third has since been added, making this series a trilogy.

The books are as follows:

- Book 1: Dad's initial entrance into the journey through serious diseases, primarily prostate cancer.
- Book 2: Having successfully beaten prostate cancer, Dad was looking forward to a period of good health. Instead, he found himself fighting bladder cancer from 2014-2017.
- Book 3: The trilogy wraps up with a chronicle of early 2018 until Dad's passing. The remainder of the book is a testament to the legacy he left behind.

Each of the books includes a section of key points from Dad's life that applies to those fighting serious illnesses. These are quick, simple guides for the reader to access when times get tough.

What the Book Is / Isn't

This book is a re-bundling of Bruce's journals from the moment he learned that he likely had prostate cancer.

The last chapter in the book is meant to be interactive: twenty-one keys to thriving have been pulled from Bruce's journals and compiled in this section. At the conclusion of each key is a blank space where you are encouraged to write notes for your current and future self. Please use this as a tool and refer back to it as often as necessary as you progress through the valley of the shadow of death.

The subtitle of the book is "A General's Strategy to Find Hope While Fighting Prostate Cancer". Bruce was fortunate to progress his career in the military to the point where he was promoted to Brigadier General. This is significant for this book for two reasons. First, Bruce was in rare company when he became general: there are only 231 generals in the U.S. Army at one time. By way of comparison, there are over 400 players in the NBA, over 1,000 players in Major League Baseball, and over 1,600 players in the NFL. This exclusivity provided Bruce with credibility as he was able to achieve something that very few people attain.

Second, as a life-long military man, he created plans, back-up plans, and back-up plans for the back-up plans. He applied this to every facet of his life, so it is not a big stretch to assume that he had plans to combat the illnesses he faced. But as you'll read, not only were those plans to combat the illness, the plans focused on how Bruce would thrive during the struggle.

That being said, Bruce would not view his battle plan as being inclusive of medical advice. This book does not offer any cures or treatments. This book is not intended to remedy your illness or symptoms.

Disclaimer

The author is not a doctor nor any type of medical professional. Bruce was not a doctor nor any type of medical professional. The following is a recording of one patient's walk through prostate cancer, thyroid issues, skin cancer occurrences, injuries sustained from a bicycle accident, and other medical issues. Nothing in this book should in any way be construed as medical advice.

This book and all that it contains is for reference only and no medical advice is offered. Consult your medical professional.

Introduction

The Inspiration

On February 18th, 2018, Bruce Wiley VanderKolk passed from this earth to his heavenly reward. His passing was sudden, shocking, and unexpected but not altogether a surprise. Bruce had cheated death many times throughout his life: he was sent to Vietnam shortly after college graduation and later in life he fought multiple battles with several different types of cancer. His family knew that the odds were in cancer's favor and that it would likely eventually prevail, claiming Bruce as yet another victim. We all realized that our time on this earth is limited and that ultimately everyone will exit this life. After watching him fight successfully against the cancers (plural intended), we thought that he had outwitted death and we would all have more time together.

But there was a history of heart attacks in his family. His father (Wiley VanderKolk) had died of a heart attack in his early 70's. His paternal grandfather (George VanderKolk) had also died of a heart attack in his early 70's. As Bruce neared that age, despite all the battles with cancer, he felt that he would break the cycle and live beyond his early 70's. Life can be cruel however. Bruce didn't make it into his mid-70's; at the time of his passing, he was coming up to his 73rd birthday.

Deep down, Bruce must have realized that his time on earth was limited, although given the above cancer wouldn't have been a prime suspect. He began chronicling his battles with cancer for two reasons. First, he used the time spent writing in introspection about his battle, trying to make sense of the suffering and illnesses. The second and more important aspect of the writing was to be a beacon for others that are (or will be) going through similar situations.

When Bruce received the initial call from his doctor in 2009 about elevated PSA levels, he began chronicling his situation in a journal he called "A Series of Events". He made a few comments to his family about the journal, but largely kept it's contents private. It wasn't until after his passing that the family discovered the extent to which Bruce recorded not just the medical happenings in his life but his feelings as well.

This book uses that journal as a foundation, including other writings of Bruce's as well as some further advice that we are sure he would have written had he not passed so soon. The journal will be divided into three specific groupings in this book: entries during his diagnosis process, entries during his treatment phase, and entries during his life after prostate cancer.

Bruce would have wanted his trials to help inspire others to not just merely survive when they are going through cancer (or some other type of life-threatening disease) but to actually thrive and to be a beacon of hope to others. While this book specifically deals with Bruce's experience with prostate cancer, the principles that Bruce journaled apply to other critical diseases as well.

Thank you for taking this journey with us. It is our hope and prayer that this book is a gift of encouragement to you or someone you know going through a difficult situation. It is also our hope and prayer that you too, can become this beacon of hope to those around you.

Bruce

The eldest of two sons, I was privileged to not only grow up in his household, but also to enjoy a close relationship with him until the day he left this earth.

Sure, there were the normal squabbles during adolescence, but in my mind they were few and far between because I saw myself as a problem-free child (I am sure that other family members would disagree with this statement, which they are free to do in their own book). It also probably helped our relationship that Dad was often out of the house, either traveling for his day job or his weekend job with the Illinois National Guard. His work with the church also took him away from the house a couple of times a month for evening meetings. If we are being completely honest, there was a healthy bit of fear in our relationship as well. Nothing straightened up a teenager like the words, "wait until your father gets home".

When I moved away to attend university in Indiana, our relationship grew stronger. The distance and not being under the same roof at the same time likely were key contributors, but I also think our relationship got stronger because Dad saw me coming into my own. I was fortunate to attend a Christian university and was blessed to form a friendship with a group of spiritually strong young men. Correction was few and far between when I was at college: Dad didn't have to worry about me partying, skipping class, carousing, drinking, etc. The strongest disagreement we had was when I was stubborn about not seeking surgery for a torn ACL because I thought it would heal on its own. After several "discussions", including a classic metaphor about an old farmer who drowned because he refused to recognize God's provision during a flood, I had the surgery. Of course Dad was right. Today, over 25 years later, the repaired knee continues to function perfectly.

I am sure that Dad had some disappointment that I didn't branch off in his career direction, but like many sons, I was determined to make my own way. Today, as I approach the age that Dad was when he took early retirement, I long to go back and follow his career path because I am still likely decades away from retirement.

Through 45 years of being his son, Dad was calm, methodical, slow to anger, eager to work with me to tackle life successfully, and many, many more adorning adjectives. My hope is that this book provides a glimpse into the man that Dad/Bruce was and that it is a blessing to your life.

But Also Dad

The reader will notice that Dad is referred to as "Bruce" throughout the majority of this book. This is intentional. The focus of the book is sharing about how Bruce was able to live an example to others while he was fighting multiple illnesses and diseases.

Bruce is the focus and rightly so. By referring to him immediately as "Dad" seems to have the effect of lessening that focus by bringing me into the situation. I am a nobody, just a man blessed to call Bruce, "Dad".

Towards the end of the book, once Bruce has been cemented into the reader's mind, you will notice an increase in the usage of the title "Dad". This is also intentional. Once "Bruce" is established, it is necessary to bring his relationship with his family back into focus because it was an important aspect of his example of thriving. This trend continues into the next book.

PART ONE

WHO WAS BRUCE VANDERKOLK?

Bruce's Life Synopsis

Michigan: The Early Years

Bruce was born on March 16th, 1945 to Wiley and Violet VanderKolk. He was the youngest of two sons. With six years between the brothers, Bruce was literally the baby of the family. The VanderKolks lived on a farm in southwest Michigan with arable farming land, but the primary focus was dairy farming. Life on a dairy farm was notoriously hard; there were no vacation days or sick days because the cows required milking twice a day, everyday. It is reasonable to believe that this lifestyle created an intense work ethic with Bruce as he grew up.

The farm was located in a remote area; the nearest large city was Grand Rapids, about an hour's drive away. The nearby towns were small and Bruce attended school in an even smaller town called Hopkins. As he struggled through the education system, Bruce aspired to go away to college, a dream that was supported by his parents. In the end he selected Michigan State University in East Lansing, MI. To him it was far enough away from home to build his independence, but near enough to go back for holiday visits.

MSU to Vietnam

Life at Michigan State University was everything Bruce hoped for: Parties, parties, and more parties. And perhaps a bit of studying. Actually, a lot more than a bit because Bruce was able to graduate with a degree in Chemistry with honors.

It was during this time that Bruce decided to focus; first a life partner. He chose wisely and renewed an earlier relationship with Donna Townsend, his eventual wife of 49 years.

The second area of focus was the developing conflict in Vietnam, specifically the consideration in the government of instituting a draft for young males, one of which was Bruce. There was the risk that he would be subject to the draft. Bruce applied his analytical mind to the options: Option 1 was to proceed ahead into the workforce and hope (and pray) that his number didn't come up in the draft. If his number did come up, then he would have to report to Basic Training and more than likely be in the Infantry.

Option 2 was to be proactive and sign up for the Reserve Officers' Training Corps (ROTC) at Michigan State. This would guarantee that he would serve in the military, but it would give him the ability to determine his path, likely away from the infantry.

Bruce chose option 2 and joined the ROTC program. Once he graduated from ROTC, it was time to report to Vietnam. He and Donna had recently married. However their time together was short lived; Bruce was going to Vietnam as an Artillery officer.

Bruce didn't speak much about his time in Vietnam, as is common with most veterans. Later in life he did do some writing about his time there, which will be the subject of future publishing works.

Post Vietnam

It isn't exactly clear when Bruce developed the habit of being proactive, but it was demonstrated in Vietnam. He started his job search before he returned to the States from his tour of duty. Similar to drafting a sleeper player that ends up being a Hall of Famer, the Illinois State Police (ISP) took a chance on the young man who applied for a chemistry position in the Forensic Science division. It probably didn't hurt his chances that he did an internship with the ISP while he was in college.

This professional relationship lasted for several decades. Bruce was instrumental in the transformation of the ISP Forensic Division from an after-thought to one of the leading departments in the entire country. He eventually retired from the ISP at a rank of Commander of the Forensic Science Division.

Bruce was obligated to continue his relationship with the US Armed Forces in the near term after his return from Vietnam. He transferred to the Army Reserves but was unable to find a spot in the contingent based in Springfield, IL. He thus transferred to the Illinois National Guard which had a spot for an officer at his level at the local base, Camp Lincoln. He rose in the ranks until he retired as a Brigadier General.

After his retirement from the Illinois State Police, Bruce was actually not ready for retirement. He lent his incredible experience of improving forensic laboratory systems to a couple of consultant projects. He even briefly considered going to Iraq to do the same, but was dissuaded by the family; Iraq in the early 2000's was not a particularly safe environment. Instead he went to work at his church in various capacities to lend his expertise in leadership and organization to improving the day-to-day operation of his church in Springfield, IL.

Cancer: The Unwanted Stalker

Bruce served faithfully in the United States Army in Vietnam, with no complaint. When the airplanes started applying chemical defoliant to the jungle surrounding the bases where he was located, there were no complaints. It was only later, much later, when he and the rest of the world came to learn the human cost of that defoliant, also known as Agent Orange, on Bruce and the thousands of other soldiers serving in Vietnam.

Cancer started to make its presence felt with Bruce in the most innocuous of circumstances: skin issues, first the ears, then the nose. Consequently, Bruce began spending quite a bit of time with a medical team in Illinois. Later in life, when he was transitioning to life in Florida, it would continue to come back, but this time required a complete face scrubbing to reduce the problem areas. The same type of face scrub that makes exposure to sun extremely painful while he was in Florida, where you can't walk outside without being exposed to direct sunlight. But, as before, he did the treatment without any complaints.

After leaving the workforce, Bruce engaged in that age-old practice of retirees everywhere: constant doctor visits to make sure that his health was on track. He was always a lover of food (particularly a good hamburger) and as a result struggled with weight, cholesterol, and pre-diabetes symptoms. It was during one of these routine visits that the doctors determined that his PSA levels were too high and may be an indication of a more serious problem.

Also during this time frame, Bruce went through issues with his thyroid. If you're not familiar with the thyroid, it is a tiny gland in your throat which produces the hormones that control many functions of the entire body. As Bruce would find out, it is not a good thing to have issues with the thyroid.

Later, Bruce would experience another, more vicious type of c-word, bladder cancer. But his writings during that fight are so extensive that another book is warranted and is the next title in this series of books.

Faith Journey

Faith's Importance to Bruce

Bruce's faith in God was the cornerstone of his life. Bruce's faith was not a static, go to church once a month, type of faith. No, his was an active faith. He believed that one of the purposes for his being on this earth was to bring more people to faith in God so that they could enjoy the benefits of everlasting life in heaven.

Faith is what drove Bruce to thrive in the face of many devastating illnesses. He clung to God's promises during dark days and he knew how he lived his life would be an example to others. He was not afraid to let others know of his faith. Bruce wrote the following synopsis of his faith journey in 2008, before his struggle with prostate cancer started.

Bruce's Personal Testimony

I grew up in the Reformed Church of America. I cannot remember a time when my parents did not faithfully go to church and take their children. I was baptized as an infant and as I grew older participated in Sunday School, Wednesday evening catechism, and Sunday night activities. When I approached high school, I joined the church and to do so I appeared before the elders to answer questions about my faith, my commitment, and biblical knowledge.

After high school I attended college and upon graduation I entered the US Army. It was during college and my initial time in the service that I became less active and committed to attending church. However, when I was sent to Vietnam I realized that I could not mentally survive unless I started again to turn my life over to God's care and providence. This time in my life was a gradual re-awakening that has continued to this day. I do not consider "the race" to be over and realize that there is much more to learn and to do in service for God. Where this will lead I do not know, however, I try to be vigilant about not closing any doors.

After military service, my wife and I attended the Presbyterian Church, the Orthodox Presbyterian Church and for the last 30 years South Side Christian Church in Springfield, IL. With each passing year I have steadily grown in my spiritual life. In June of 1978 I was baptized by immersion. After studying the scriptures I could not see where baptism is proclaimed in the Bible except by immersion.

I have served as a deacon and several years as an elder at South Side Christian Church. I have taught several years of Adult Bible School and have assisted in several other ministries of the church. After retiring from the Illinois State Police in 2001, I went to work at South Side Christian Church as the Church Administrator. I later moved into the Equipping and Assimilating ministry on a part time basis. In April 2010, after the Senior Minister left, I served as the Executive Minister overseeing the staff and ministers. I have participated in providing training to other elders or potential elders on the practical aspects of being an elder and other leadership issues. This has been done at South Side Christian Church, Restoration House Ministries in New Hampshire, and at Maritime Christian College in Prince Edward Island.

I have gone through many personal challenges in addition to my Vietnam experience. I have gone through Donna's cancer over 20 years ago, a stroke by our youngest son while he was in high school, personal injuries and cancer resulting in 10 major surgeries. I have experienced the "highs and lows" that come with these. I have several times asked God why? Through all of this my faith has grown but I am not where I should be. God has been good and I have been blessed. I believe the following two statements:

"God is good all the time. All the time God is good."

"The storms of our life prove the strength of our Anchor."

Bruce W. VanderKolk (April 21, 2008, revised September 23, 2015)

Bruce's Faith in God and His Service (written by Bruce VanderKolk)

1. Grew up going to the Reformed Church in Bradley, MI
    a. Was sprinkled in junior high school and had catechism classes at that time

2. *Attended 1st Presbyterian Church in Joliet, IL 1969*
   a. *Part of a small group, and attended a retreat at Stronghold, Oregon, IL*
3. *Presbyterian Church in Geneseo, IL 1970-1973*
4. *Orthodox Presbyterian Church in Wheaton, IL 1973-1977*
   a. *Headed up the nursery*
5. *South Side Christian Church, Springfield, IL 1978-2011*
   a. *Immersed June of 1978*
   b. *Sponsor of Bible Bowl*
   c. *Deacon*
   d. *Elder*
   e. *Chairman of Elders*
   f. *Bible School Teacher*
      i. *U&I Class – College age Students*
      ii. *Adult Bible School classes*
   g. *Church Administrator – Paid Position 2001-2006*
   h. *Assimilation and Equip Coordinator*
   i. *Executive Minister 2010*
   j. *Volunteered at homeless shelter*
6. *Attended Church of God, Oregon, IL*
   a. *Volunteered at homeless shelter*
7. *Anchor Christian Church, Bonita Springs, FL 2013-2018*
   a. *Elder*
   b. *Chairman of Missions Committee*
   c. *On building committee*
   d. *Chairman of 55+ ministry*
   e. *Adult Bible School teacher*

PART TWO

HOW THEN TO THRIVE?

Faith: The Foundation to the Path Forward

As you will read throughout the remainder of this book, Bruce relied on his faith as he faced one serious illness after another. Bruce spent countless hours throughout his life reading and studying the Bible. He came to the conclusion that for those that have faith in Him, God will not fail His children.

Following are two essays that Bruce wrote regarding his faith. The first essay was written during his battle with bladder cancer, but the message is timeless and applies to his earlier diseases as well. The second is a reflection of the impact that his time in Vietnam played on his faith.

These two essays speak to the importance of faith for Bruce while he faced very different life-threatening situations.

"He will not fail us" (Bruce)

Psalm 91 (NIV)

1 Whoever dwells in the shelter of the Most High
will rest in the shadow of the Almighty.
2 I will say of the Lord, "He is my refuge and my fortress,
my God, in whom I trust."
3 Surely he will save you
From the fowler's snare
and from the deadly pestilence.
4 He will cover you with his feathers,
and under his wings you will find refuge;
his faithfulness will be your shield and rampart.
5 You will not fear the terror of night,
Nor the arrow that flies by day,
6 nor the pestilence that stalks in the darkness,
Nor the plague that destroys at midday.

7 A thousand may fall at your side,
ten thousand at your right hand,
but it will not come near you.
8 You will only observe with your eyes
and see the punishment of the wicked.
9 If you say, "The Lord is my refuge,"
and you make the Most High your dwelling,
10 no harm will overtake you,
no disaster will come near your tent.
11 For he will command his angels concerning you
to guard you in all your ways;
12 they will lift you up in their hands,
so that you will not strike your foot against a stone.
13 You will tread on the lion and the cobra;
you will trample the great lion and the serpent.
14 "Because he loves me," says the Lord, "I will rescue him;
I will protect him, for he acknowledges my name.
15 He will call on me, and I will answer him;
I will be with him in trouble,
I will deliver him and honor him.
16 With long life I will satisfy him
and show him my salvation."

I am always amazed when those who have cancer outwardly appear to have a tranquil nature. I wish I could copy that DNA of tranquility into my own mind and personality. Maybe they are at peace with their situation and the outward appearance is real and not a brave front. Unfortunately, my situation has been displayed as that of a chameleon. To others I change my color to reflect an appearance of strength and acceptance. I try not to take the cancer seriously in front of others and when asked I reply, "I'm doing ok". I live a life externally of pretending that nothing really is wrong and a philosophy of "this too will pass- no big deal".

But it is a big deal; I just do not want to admit it outwardly. Besides, I have found that many people who have not experienced the trials of cancer do not want to talk about it, do not understand the emotions a person goes through, may even avoid you as if you have leprosy. My situation may even remind them of their own personal experience of cancer or of someone who had cancer and they do not want to bring to surface from the depths of inner parts of their mind the pain that they have gone through. This is where my other chameleon color comes in.

When alone my mind is in turmoil; it is constantly making my daily life one of contrasts, like a yo-yo that is ever moving up and down. One moment I may be up and the next I may be at the bottom of the yo-yo's cycle; a cycle that is in perpetual motion denying the laws of physics. I am in a 24/7 mode of operation as there appears no escape from the reality of cancer. It is there with you when you wake up; it is there with you in the morning hours; it is there with you when you go to the store; it is there with you when you may be entertaining; it is there with you when you're watching television at night; it is there with you when you go to bed and you pray to God for healing; it is there when for some reason you wake up during the night; it is always present, never ending. How do you explain that to someone who has not walked in the same shoes and does not have a grasp of the terrible experiences that cancer brings? In some ways, I think the mental aspects of dealing with cancer may be as bad or worse then the physical aspects of dealing with cancer.

I wish I had a magic formula to give you as you go through many trials, but I do not. Well-intended people may say "just rely upon God", "out of adversity there comes good", "I know you will be ok", or "there are a lot of new treatments today that will help you". Well, thanks but this does not help. Sure, I appreciate their sincerity and attempts at giving hope, but words alone do not provide peace of mind; words do not heal.

I may sound cynical and maybe I am to some extent. However, as I have tried to come to grips with my cancer, I know I could not continue without drawing upon the strength given to us through our belief in God and the many comforting verses found in His Word. Does it totally solve my daily mental gyrations; no, but I cannot imagine what it would be like without His love and care for me to minimize those gyrations. I wonder how do those with cancer who do not have a relationship with God ever make it through the day? Where is their hope? The answer is they have no hope! You see I believe God truly understands my situation. And I fully understand that my way may not be His way.

There are many great Bible verses that give comfort and strength. Some of my favorites are found in the book of Philippians, such as:

"Rejoice in the Lord always. I will say it again: Rejoice! Let your gentleness be evident to all. The Lord is near. Do not be anxious about anything, but in everything, by prayer and petition, with thanks-giving, present your requests to God. And the peace of God, which transcends all understanding, will guard your *hearts and your minds in Christ Jesus. Finally, brothers, whatever is true, whatever is noble, whatever is right, whatever is pure, whatever is lovely, whatever is admirable-if anything is excellent or praiseworthy-think about such things. Whatever you have learned or received or heard from me, or seen in me-put it into practice. And the God of peace will be with you." Philippians 4:4-9 (NIV).*

And:

"Forgetting what is behind and straining toward what is ahead, I press on toward the goal to win the prize for which God has called me heavenward in Christ Jesus." Philippians 3:13b-14 (NIV).

Finally, I return to the scripture quoted at the beginning of this writing, Psalm 91 (NIV): A Psalm of hope and comfort. How can we not find solace when we read the following about God?

- *we will rest in the shadow of the Almighty*
- *He is my refuge and my fortress, ... in whom I trust*
- *He will save you*
- *He will cover you with his feathers*
- *under His wings you will find refuge*
- *His faithfulness will be your shield and rampart*
- *He will command his angels concerning you to guard you in all your ways*
- *He will protect you, when we acknowledge His name.*
- *He will be with you in trouble*
- *He will deliver you and honor you*

Do I expect my life to be a "bed of roses" because I put my trust in His words of hope and comfort? No. Do I expect that this life will pass away and there will be a more glorious life for eternity with our Lord and Savior? Yes.

May you seek comfort in knowing that what is coming is far greater than what you are going through now.

Bruce W. VanderKolk (5 November 2017)

How I Saw God's Faithfulness Through a War Situation

When I was asked to apply how the question of "how God is faithful?" to my experiences in Vietnam, I thought it was quite easy. In fact, I said it could be summed up in three words-"I came back". However, upon further reflection, I am not sure that this is an appropriate answer. I'm not sure because it could be implied that those who did not come back were unfaithful. I'm not sure it is an appropriate answer because God does not say that we will not encounter difficulties or even death. The more I pondered the question, the more difficult it was to find an answer.

Actually, the question of how we see God's faithfulness has nothing to do with a war situation. It could just as easily be applied to our work, a vacation, a sporting event or even here at the church. It does not matter what your setting, God is faithful to those who are faithful to him. He is faithful according to His plan, not ours. His faithfulness is shown by the fulfillment of His promises.

When I went to Vietnam, I had to realize I was not in control but that I had to put my trust in God. Once that happened, I was at peace. No longer did I fear the potential terrible consequences of war or death. And why? Because we are protected by the power of God and he will provide a spiritual deliverance according to his plan, not necessarily a physical deliverance.

If I was to modify the question, I would ask "How did I experience God's promises as a result of His faithfulness to me in a war situation". I experienced His promises in several ways. The most prominent were:

- An inner peace
- Strength to face another day
- Confidence
- Comfort
- Boldness
- Assurance
- Courage
- Encouragement
- Answered prayer

One way God comforts me I believe is by sending the words to songs into my mind and then the constant rhythmical repetition of the verses. One of these is the song "He Lives" by Gloria and Bill Gaither. The lyrics of the third verse of that song explains the peace of mind I felt. The verse speaks to the glory that we will

23

experience when we leave this life and enter heaven because of the gift delivered as a result of Jesus overcoming death. Because of Jesus and his sacrifice, we will one day live forever and ever with God.

Is God faithful in a war situation? Yes

But the more important question is "Is God faithful at all times?"

The answer is Yes.

Bruce W. VanderKolk

Sometime between 2001 and 2005

Thriving

Life is Hard (Roger)

One of the most over-used phrases is that "Life is Hard". It generally is followed by a second phrase such as "get up" or "suck it up" that is meant to encourage the listener to overcome the hardness of life.

The reality is that yes, Life is Hard. Period. End of Story. A bit of faith coming in, but if you are a believer, the Bible makes it plain as day that life isn't a bed of roses. Sin has entered our world and we will never experience a life that is truly easy. Sure, we will all experience times of peace, but during those times, the universe is in the background planning, plotting, and scheming on how to bring pain, loss, or something equally as devastating back into our lives.

Psychology tells us that there are five stages of grief: Denial, Anger, Bargaining, Depression, and Acceptance. When we are faced with life-changing, devastating news, we will all go through these stages, ending at acceptance.

But after acceptance, we must still figure out how to move on with life. In the face of severe adversity, we have three options as to how we will proceed:

1. We can surrender. We can give up and let the disease win. We can withdraw from society, friends, family and wait for the disease to achieve its ultimate goal of defeating the body.
2. We can survive. We can only do what is necessary to come out of the other side of the disease. We can throw all of the strength and resources that we can pull together to beat the disease.
3. We can thrive. Building upon the choice to survive, we can fight the disease. We can also work to ensure that our lives enrich those around us, whether it be family, friends, acquaintances, or society as a whole.

We must choose. The bad news is that life isn't fair: once we make a decision to choose one option such as to Thrive, life will continue to tempt us to change our minds. Even those who decide to Thrive will face the option of surrendering.

Despite all of the hardness that life threw at him, Bruce made the decision to Thrive.

What it Means to Thrive

Whenever we are faced with a difficult situation, the immediate focus is just to survive the episode so that we can live to fight another day. There is absolutely nothing wrong with pursuing the survival path because it is valid: as finite creatures, we need to make sure that we do everything in our power to extend our life on this earth.

The problem comes when the survival path is the only path we choose. When the focus is solely on survival, after we are successful there is no further action moving forward. This is limiting, not only for the person going through the battle, but for society as a whole.

Webster defines the word "thrive" as: "to grow or develop successfully; to flourish or succeed; to progress toward or realize a goal despite or because of circumstances."

As he fought through his battles with cancer and other diseases, Bruce came to realize that there are two types of thriving:

1. Thriving Internally - The first stage of thriving is learning how to flourish in spite of difficult circumstances. How to wake up in the morning and get out of bed. How to get the head and emotions in a good spot.
2. Thriving Externally - The second stage is taking the internal flourishing and packaging it as a tool to help others. Thriving is the act of blessing the lives of others. It is focusing not on yourself and your difficult situation, but focusing on how to improve the lives of others.

As you begin reading through what is essentially Bruce's journals, you will see his path transform from one of survival to one that promoted both internal and external thriving. Whether he consciously realized it or not, Bruce's path became a source of blessing for others, helping those around him going through battles to flourish despite or because of circumstances.

It is my goal to share his journey with the masses to increase the blessing of his journey through multiple struggles.

PART THREE

BRUCE'S JOURNEY

Diagnosis

May 12- June, 2009 (Bruce)

It seemed like a routine day on May 12, 2009 except that I was scheduled for my annual physical. My only concern was the cholesterol, triglycerides, high and low lipids reading. As usual I did not have anything to eat from 6:00p the day before and looked forward to having a breakfast afterwards.

Later in the afternoon I received a call that my cholesterol was 170mg/dl, triglycerides 130 mg/dl, LDL 115 mg/dl and HDL 36 mg/dl. All were excellent except that the HDL was a little low. However, my PSA was 7.210 ng/ml (reference range is 0-4.900). This news was disturbing. For the past few years my PSA had gradually been rising and approximately two years ago I had a biopsy which proved to be negative (at that time I was slightly above 5.0).

As a result of this new reading, I was scheduled to see a doctor that I had seen previously when my PSA started to increase and every six months afterwards. This was set for June 5, 2009. I proceeded to do a lot of research on the Internet about prostate cancer and procedures if it proved to actually be cancer. The time, however, was constantly filled with thoughts that I was sure it was cancer and I begin to think about what would be the best option. None of the options are good as the side effects can be troublesome. For whatever reason, I just assumed the worst and that the prostate would show cancer. This was not how I had planned my future. I had always been afraid of the long term lingering effects that cancer can cause and the loss of the dignity of life. My plan had always been to die of a heart attack like my dad. Quick and with no long drawn-out process.

I was angry but not sure what about or who I should direct my anger at. In my mind I knew that I could not dictate the outcome. If it was cancer, I had the same old question as most other people: Why me? I don't think I was mad at God as much as I was about not being able to do many of the physical activities that I do now (again I assumed the worst). I had been working all year on biking over 3,000 miles and was closing in on 2,000 before the end of June. I loved to bike and feel the countryside move past me. It was the one exercise that I could do somewhat well. I had difficulty walking long distances as I fell from a roof in August of 2000 and ended up with a Lisfranc injury (this tore all five metatarsal

29

bones out of the socket in my left foot and it never healed properly). I did not want to face the future being inactive or only moderately active.

Prior to June 5th I received a call from the medical facility that my visit needed to be rescheduled. The next available date that worked for me was June 11th. Thus the uncertainty continued and all of the negative imaginations of the potential risk of cancer continued.

Finally, June 11th came and I saw the doctor. It was a very fast visit as the doctor felt that I should have a more extensive biopsy than what I had before. Thus I was scheduled for surgery on the 24th of June at the local medical facility. During this procedure the doctor would take between 20-30 samples to examine. The previous biopsy was only 8 samples as that is the most that could be taken without being put under general anesthesia. However, before they would do the surgery I had to have a pre-op physical. This was to be done by another doctor.

On June 22, 2009, I went in for the pre-op physical. This also held a surprise for me as my EKG was abnormal. The doctor looked at my computerized history and also found that an EKG prior to my shoulder surgery in March of 2008 also had an abnormal EKG. However, neither the doctor nor myself were ever informed about the March abnormality. The doctor scheduled me to see another doctor, on June 23, 2009 as this issue needed to be resolved prior to surgery on the 24th. This doctor examined the EKG and offered as an explanation that possibly I had a mild heart attack sometime in mid-2007 to March of 2008. The reason for the time frame was that the doctor had done a stress test and EKG in July of 2007 and approved me to climb Pikes Peak. The following EKG's were pronounced in their abnormality and they were consistent. Because the EKG had not changed since 2008, the doctor approved me for the surgery on the 24th however the doctor scheduled me for a follow-up nuclear stress test and ECHO on 28 July. This would allow sufficient time for healing from the surgery on the 24th. The doctor did advise there is always a possibility of a heart attack during the surgery but it was remote.

During the examination, the doctor noticed a growth on my Thyroid. This is really what I needed, a third thing to be concerned about. I was referred back to the original doctor and had an appointment in the afternoon of the same day. This doctor also felt the growth and scheduled me for an ultrasound thyroid test on Monday, June 29th.

June, 2009

In retrospect, I can see why we did not plan on another summer trip to Colorado. I would have had to cancel. I do not believe this was a coincidence but God working in my life (I am not sure why or how these issues all fit into His plan but I suspect this will be known sometime in the near or far future either by me or someone else).

The Importance of Research (Roger)

In the old spy movies, there would undoubtedly be a scene where an unsuspecting person would be told to "trust no one". There is a similar phrase dealing with trust in the military: Trust but verify.

Bruce trusted what his doctors told him. But having an analytical mind and spending many years in the military, he decided to verify through his own research.

The Internet is a fantastic tool for patients such as Bruce. The amount of information available is tremendous. Bruce would be at his computer for hours on end researching this potential foe. With any tool, there is potential for pitfalls with using the Internet solely as an information source.

Useful Tool:
- Information increases the confidence in decision-making.
- Provides clarity to know what to expect.
- Connect with others that have gone through a similar situation.

Potential pitfalls:
- Quickens the onset and increases the severity of worry: The more we know, the more there is for us to be afraid of.
- Contains erroneous information which is not a firm foundation to use for treatment or quality of life plans.
- Lessens the urgency to seek counsel from a professional.

Bottom line: Trust your doctor, but verify.

---

1 July 2009 (Bruce)

Today I received word back on my biopsy and ultrasound.

The results were: I have "prostatic intraepithelial neoplasia" ("PIN"). It appears to be a pre-cancer condition which frequently leads to cancer but not always. A neighbor had been found to have PIN in Jan/Feb and then in April they found cancer. We meet with the doctor on the 16th when we get back in town to discuss what to do next. From what I can find out at this time, at the minimum, it will lead to frequent PSA tests and a biopsy at 3 or 6 months intervals.

My thyroid results came back and I have nodules on both sides of the thyroid. There are a lot of reasons for this and cancer is one possibility among others. One of the principle causes of thyroid cancer is exposure to radiation. As a teenager I had extensive exposure to radiation as one of the treatments back then for acne was radiation. This technique was listed as a cause for adult thyroid cancer. I am scheduled to meet with another doctor on the 27th of July about this.

As you can see the news is not very positive but not totally negative. There is still a lot to be determined. From what I see on the Internet, a high grade of PIN is a pretty strong predictor of cancer at some point in time. The other question is whether or not I may in fact have cancer but the areas selected were only PIN. Apparently you can find both at the same time. I have been scheduled to see the doctor on July 16th to discuss the results and to determine a plan for the future.

The thyroid results were not a surprise-if they can feel a growth, then one should show up. However, I am surprised at the fact that nodules were present on both sides. Again, there are a lot of possibilities as to the cause and cancer is only one answer. They could also be benign. I see this doctor on July 27th. I have the nuclear heart test on the 28th.

It has been good being in Oregon, IL as I have people around who have been keeping me busy. In Springfield I do not have the same distractions.

I emailed our minister and gave him the OK to inform the staff. I see no reason to keep this now quiet. In fact, it does help to talk about it and keeping silent isn't going to help me. Talking about it may help someone else in the future who experiences the same situation.

I told Marv (brother) and Roger (son) that I am in the process of dodging bullets. Hopefully I dodge right when I should, left when I should, and stay put when I should. What this really means is that the information I am told by the doctors and their guidance will help me make the right choice. This is also my prayer-that God directs the doctors and me in making the right choice.

2 July 2009

After finding this out I am much more at ease with what is going on and I think I am coping better. I should not take the credit as the credit goes to God. I am not angry at this time. If God wants me to be free from cancer or if it is cancer and wants me to be healed, then that is what will happen. I can even joke about it but in an odd way, e.g. I told Donna today that Jamie (son) said he has first dibbs on the GMC truck! He didn't really say that.

In some ways I am beginning to sense that this period of time may be more difficult on those who are near me, my family. I need to pray for them. The uncertainty of the future in many ways parallels the uncertainty of when I boarded the plane in Grand Rapids, Michigan, back in 1968 to go to Vietnam. Sure I was scared but I think it is easier on the person going through a trial then those who are near you

A friend from church sent an email today with a touching attachment. I have printed it off. It was very timely. It is called "Now that's God." God passes us through tribulation to see a brighter day. It's just that at the present moment we do not understand and find it difficult to envision the brighter day. I did not interpret the statement that God deliberately causes these situations to occur but that He can take us through the tribulation to a brighter tomorrow.

The card ended with:

"DO YOU THINK THAT THIS CARD WAS ACCIDENTALLY SENT TO YOU?
NOPE!"

The card was timely and I do not think it was just a coincidence.

Intercessory Prayer (Roger)

Did you catch that important couple of sentences in the previous journal? Bruce wrote "In some ways I am beginning to sense that this period of time may be more difficult on those who are near me, my family. I need to pray for them…I think it is easier on the person going through a trial than those who are near you."

Wow. What a deep level of clarity at the dynamics of the battle that he was going through. He knew that his family was praying fervently for him. But he also saw fit to pray for his family. Why? He knew that we were all going to be in the struggle against cancer together.

Perhaps this came from his military training and his lifelong career in the military. If you've listened to any soldier speak of their experience in a combat zone, they will all speak to their goal of fighting not so much for their country, but for their brother or sister next to them in the fight. This concept is known as a "battle buddy" or a "swim buddy" in the Navy SEAL's. Quite simply, the purpose of the concept is to increase the performance of the soldier by making them responsible and accountable to a fellow soldier.

Whether he realized it or not, Bruce was adapting this military concept to his civilian life and the struggle that he was engaged in against cancer. He knew that his family was praying for him but he also took it upon himself to pray for his family so that they might endure and overcome the struggle as well.

This is such a simple concept but arguably one that is overlooked as we fight the struggles of life. All of us go through valleys in life: cancer, loss of a job, other serious illnesses, divorce, loss of a child, etc. When we are in those valleys, we are usually bathed in prayer from our friends, families, church members, etc. Helping others when they are struggling is foundational to our relationships.

But how often do we turn the tables and pray for the other person? How often do we approach the throne of God and ask for strength for the other person as they walk through this valley with us?

If you're going through a struggle while you're reading this book, chances are good that you are being prayed for by someone else. But who are you praying for? Take a minute and consider which of your friends or family members is actively supporting you with thoughts and prayers. You'll both be strengthened when you return the favor.

Who is your battle buddy?

---

13 July 2009 (Bruce)

As I was driving to the elder's meeting tonight, for some reason I thought about Vietnam and the parallel to what I am going through now. In Vietnam, we received numerous 107mm rocket rounds. Sometimes you could hear them coming in and other times you did not know about them until they hit the ground and exploded. We always "joked" about when one of these would have our name on it. Some of the times the rockets did not hit near us as the aiming process used was not the most accurate by the Vietcong. However, there were sufficient instances where they would hit relatively close and at times we would be spared because of the sand bags piled around us-obviously the sand bags would not have helped in a direct hit.

I see the three situations I am going through as three rocket rounds aimed at me. Maybe they will miss by some distance; maybe they may be relatively close; or maybe one of the three may actually hit me and cause a life-altering path.

As I learned in Vietnam, I should not worry about being hit because if I did I would be ineffective and probably go crazy. The same is true now; I cannot worry about these things that I cannot control. I can only ask God to protect me as He did in Vietnam if that is His will.

In the closed session tonight of the elder's meeting the minister brought up to the others about my situation. I'm glad he did as I was not sure how to bring up the issue. I feel comfortable talking about the issue but I can see where others do not know what to say or how to act. They did pray for me in the closing prayer and I appreciate that.

15 July 2009

As I was reading Luke tonight in reference to the Trinity, I found in Luke 18:1 where Jesus tells his disciples that they should always pray and not give up. I think this is a great message and timely; pray and do not give up.

"Then Jesus told his disciples a parable to show them that they should always pray and not give up." (NIV)

16 July 2009

Today we met with the doctor about the results of my biopsy and PIN ("Prostatic Intraepithelial Neoplasia" - Basically an indication of a pre-malignant condition). I'm not sure it was all that informative as the doctor didn't provide much information. It seems that this time and the last time I saw the doctor they were in a hurry and anxious to move on to someone else. I am glad I came prepared with some questions. The questions and the response follows:

- *Was the PIN low grade or high grade? Answer: High grade*
- *How many samples contained PIN? Answer: Only found PIN on one side and not in all of the samples on that side (10 total were done)*
- *Was the doctor certain there was no PC ("Prostate Cancer") in the prostate or these samples? Did not ask that question because the doctor had stated previously that prostate cancer is a hit and miss proposition-it is at the cellular level unlike a tumor that might appear someplace else.*
- *Does PIN affect the PSA level? ("Prostate-Specific Antigen" - Protein produced by tissue in the prostate used to indicate potential presence of cancer) Answer: Yes (Note: some places I found online indicated PIN does not affect PSA!)*
- *What are the chances of finding PC if another biopsy is done? Answer: That it is a hit or miss so might hit it if PC was present or might miss it*
- *Is PIN a precursor to PC? Answer: This is still an unknown. The doctor indicated there is a lot that is still unknown about prostate cancer.*
- *Does diet impact PIN? Some thought that it might affect either PIN or PC. Answer: The doctor suggested eating tomatoes.*
- *Any clinical trials on PIN? Answer: Not that the doctor is aware of. I found that odd as a national cancer site I found had many listed clinical trials going on, some closed but some still open.*
- *Prevention Chemo? Answer: Not aware of it. The doctor said if giving chemo was tried, the doctor would be hung up? Again I found that interesting as it seem to be fairly well known on websites that I saw.*
- *How quickly could PC develop? Answer: Didn't really answer this question. I mentioned about the neighbor's situation-PIN in Jan or Feb, PC in April, a lot when prostate removed in August. The doctor indicated that PC was probably present in Jan but not found.*
- *Course of Action? Answer: PSA in 3 months and will see after that what to do next.*
- *Can biking increase PSA? Answer: Yes, any irritation of the prostate can increase PSA*

The doctor did not think it would be a good idea to have another biopsy at this time as the prostate is still inflamed and it would be difficult to analyze the samples. Overall I had the impression that the doctor was nonchalant about the issue, as if it is not a huge concern at this time. Of course the doctor is not the one facing the issue!

27 July 2009

Saw a doctor this afternoon about my thyroid. Took about an hour and at this point not very encouraging. I have a growth in the center which is about 2cm (about ¾ of an inch), one on the right side about 1.3 cm and another on the left about 1.2 cm. There are also other smaller ones. I am scheduled for a biopsy Monday at the local medical facility for at least the three larger nodules (needle biopsy). There are three possible outcomes: 1) benign, 2) indeterminable, in which case they probably will repeat the biopsy, possibly the same way or actual surgery in which they will cut into the throat and the growths to take samples, and 3) it is cancer, in which case they would remove the thyroid and also probably check lymph nodes to see if it has spread.

Hard to believe but these just didn't grow overnight. I wonder how long it has been in process. Also hard to believe it was found by chance, e.g. an abnormal EKG in prep for prostate biopsy (I do not believe in chance: for everything there is a reason and a purpose of which we do not know the answer, but God does. In time it may be revealed to us.) Also, if I had the prostate biopsy done at the medical facility and not under general anesthesia, as I did the first time, I would not have had the EKG and we still would not know about it. Lots of choices have been made to arrive at this point.

From what I can find out from doing research online, there are five types of thyroid cancer. These are:

1. Papillary thyroid cancer. The papillary type of thyroid cancer is the most common, making up about 80 percent of all thyroid cancer diagnoses. Papillary thyroid cancer can occur at any age, but is most commonly diagnosed in people ages 30 to 50.

2. Follicular thyroid cancer. Follicular thyroid cancer also includes Hurthle cell cancer. Follicular thyroid cancer typically occurs in people older than 50.

3. Medullary thyroid cancer. Medullary thyroid cancer may be associated with inherited genetic syndromes that include tumors in other glands. Most medullary thyroid cancers are sporadic, meaning they aren't associated with inherited genetic syndromes.

4. Anaplastic thyroid cancer. The anaplastic type of thyroid cancer is very

rare, aggressive and very difficult to treat. Anaplastic thyroid cancer typically occurs in people age 60 or older.

5. *Thyroid lymphoma. Thyroid lymphoma begins in the immune system cells in the thyroid.*

I must admit these are trying times. It is difficult to remain at an emotional high and to pretend that all is well. I guess that at this time I cope best by remaining very active. I have started back into biking which will help and today went 33 miles. However, somehow it would be nice to have my brain switch the thought of these issues off. Very difficult not to find yourself thinking about the three "rockets" that need to be dodged.

28 July 2009

Had the Nuclear Stress test and Echo Cardiogram this morning. Seemed to go ok and I had no discomfort from the tests. Now we wait, again, for the results.

Power of Music (Roger)

Our family was small: Dad, Mom, and two sons. We were fortunate and blessed to have the type of relationship where we genuinely loved and cared for each other. As adults, even though we were spread out geographically, we tried to get together as often as possible because we loved spending time together. If physical travel was not possible, then there were multiple phone calls throughout the week to check in and see how everyone was doing.

I write that to make the following admission: Bruce was pretty successful in hiding the level of despondency that he described in the preceding pages. There was definitely a lot of despair within him regarding this suffering, suffering in which he was an unwilling participant. Perhaps it was because we viewed him as the powerful head of the household that we didn't make a big deal of asking how he was doing, mentally and emotionally. Yes, he was going through some medical scares, but in our minds he was mentally fit and capable of beating all of the issues in as short of time as possible. Perhaps it was just because he had two sons who didn't understand the importance of following up with words, questions, and conversations to ascertain his emotional state. We, unfortunately, learn depth and compassion through experience.

You will notice as the battle increases in the coming months that Bruce continues to turn to Scripture to seek out God for comfort, encouragement, and guidance for the path forward. He was in tune with the written word and made regular use of it during his journey.

We were unable to convince Dad to embrace the power found in modern Christian music. The industry has come a long way from the times of the hymns of old; much of the music being produced today speaks directly to the relationship of mankind to their Heavenly Father. Please don't misunderstand: Scripture is important. Vital. Music is secondary. But music can be an important aspect of healing and getting through the battles that life throws at us.

Since college back in the 1990's, I have been drawn to music and lyrics. The actual playing of notes with the music and the singing pulls it all together, but I've felt that the lyrics are where the actual power is found. Good song lyrics contain the power and promise of God for our lives.

There are many, many, many songs which speak directly to the hearts of the troubled. One such song was released by the artist David Crowder in 2021 that would have spoken directly to Bruce's feelings by reminding him that all brokenness is only temporary. The song is "Hallelujah for Every Broken Heart". Search for the song lyrics online and read through the lyrics. Then read them again. If you're going through struggles, read them again. Print out the lyrics and post them in a location that you will be able to reflect often on the power of coming closer to God during the struggles.

As much as we all would do everything in our power to change Dad's struggles, there is a truth that faith is made stronger during these times when our heart is broken. Often our growth is strongest when we perceive all things are lost. As you continue to read through Dad's journal, it is evident that his faith was increased throughout his struggle.

What is not noted in his journal is the strengthening of faith of his family, friends, and even acquaintances who were aware of Dad's struggle. The example that Dad provided during this time helped us come closer to God not only during his struggle, but also for the remainder of our life.

Life's struggles break our bodies, our minds, our emotions, and our hearts. But thanks be to God for the growth in our relationship with Him that develop through these struggles.

---

29 July 2009 (Bruce)

After dinner I started to have a slight headache and at around 8:00p I took my blood pressure. It was 170/97 which is high. Also felt different but hard to explain. Donna was gone and thought about calling her but decided to wait. Took it about 45 min later and it was up to 188/101. Now I know something is not right as it should not be going up if all I am doing is watching TV.

Donna finally came home and convinced me to call the local medical facility. Explained the situation to the nurse on call and a doctor was notified. The doctor said I should go to emergency. Went there and after blood tests, CT Scan and X-rays they did not find anything wrong. At about 12:15am blood pressure had gone down and they let me go home. Got home about 1:00am.

30 July 2009

Received call from the doctor's nurse that Stress Test was ok. No results yet from the Echo. However, because of last night's high blood pressure the doctor wanted to see me. Appointment set up for 12:15p today. Also blood pressure this morning at 7:08 was 144/82 but at 10:12 it had gone up to 166/96. Also had slight headache again. Something obviously is going on as this is unusual-stress related?

The doctor said my stress test and echo were normal although one area was low normal. This is where the bottom part of the heart pumps out the blood and creates a vacuum which helps bring in new blood. If lower, the vacuum pressure will not circulate as much blood and oxygen to the body. Thus I might get tired or winded sooner. However, the doctor said to continue to exercise moderately but stay away from high intensity exercise. The doctor gave me some additional tablets to help lower the blood pressure and a tablet to take if the blood pressure again gets above 165/100 but only take it once. The doctor wants to see me in a month.

Life can sure change in a heartbeat. Fine one day and then the next day things start to go to pot, even though at that point you still feel good. I have a feeling this is a point in time of my life where some major adjustments will be made, e.g. losing weight, watching what I eat and who knows what else. Had breakfast this morning with a close friend as another friend had told him about some of my problems. We discussed what is important in life and what kind of a legacy or memorial do we want to be remembered by. I guess if I was to offer any advice to younger people it would be to keep their priorities straight. God first then family. After that nothing is really all that important. I have tried to do that but have not always succeeded. Who will remember, or even care, that I was a General in the Army National Guard or Commander of Forensic Science for the Illinois State Police? The real important issue is what will my family remember about me and what will other people remember about me? All of my collections and memorabilia are meaningless. What did I do to help my family and what did I do to help other people? Back to the advice to younger people I am sure they will not understand and must go through the "life of experience" before reality hits home. Remember the saying "Too old soon and too late smart."

I think the high blood pressure was maybe stress related.

Overall the results of the heart tests were good news. I guess one rocket has been diverted.

August 3, 2009

Thyroid biopsy done this morning by a doctor at the local medical facility. Took about 40 minutes and they took eight samples from the largest growth. The doctor thought by looking at the sonogram that it would be benign. Somewhat sore but not bad. Now we wait for the results.

A Change: Intended or Happenstance? (Roger)

While pulling the information from Bruce's journal over to this book, I noticed a slight change in how he was recording the dates of the entries. Prior to August, the format was date, month, year, with no commas. After August, he switched his format to a month, date, year format with a comma between the month and the year. This is weird because Bruce was a creature of habit.

Was this just an unconscious change or was he starting to realize the validity of his journal for other people and began to make the formatting more official? We will not know the answer to this question this side of heaven of course, but it is an interesting change.

August 7, 2009 (Bruce)

The biopsy showed that the growth was benign. I really did not know how to react. I was certain that it would come back positive as this was the "why" of the series of events. It was good and unexpected news. Thank God for the results. He is not done with me yet. Need to have a follow up in December to see if there is any change in the growth.

October 8, 2009

Just leave me alone. Just when I started to feel comfortable about what has been going on I noticed a large growth on my neck, about where you would expect the thyroid gland to be. I am confident that it was not there earlier in the summer because after the doctor found the growth I could not see it. I met with another doctor on October 7th and a sonogram was scheduled for that afternoon. I am scheduled to see the doctor tomorrow to find out the results, e.g. is it actually growing?

Today I received a call from another doctor's nurse that the results from the PSA test which I had on Monday were up to 8.04. The doctor wants to do another biopsy. This is scheduled for Nov 5, 2009 at the local medical facility

I really am getting tired of these oscillating cycles of bad news-good news-bad news. I am starting to have a better appreciation for others who go through these cycles. Even when you get good news, the prior bad news does not go away immediately (if ever). Over time, however, the bad news does start to dissipate but it is always in the back of your mind. To pretend that it has no effect is impossible, at least to me. One does eventually accept the bad news but when it turns to good news you just wonder for how long. It's like waiting and wondering when the next bomb will drop.

This morning I told Donna at least this time we are only dealing with two bullets as the heart bullet has been put down.

Oscillating Cycles (Roger)

At his core, Bruce was a scientist so of course he would use the term "oscillating cycle" rather than something generic as "ups and downs".

But he was 100% spot on with his take on the frustrations of cycling between good news and bad news. The constant cycling is exhausting: We function best during periods of stability because stability enables our brains to focus on more important tasks rather than having to fret about whether the immediate future is clear or murky.

As you continue reading his journal, this frustration will continue to surface as Bruce struggled to put his troubles behind him so that he can focus on thriving in the midst of his path.

October 9, 2009 (Bruce)

Saw the doctor this morning and my thyroid growth has not changed much since last time. Therefore the doctor recommends not removing it at this time but instead doing another test in April. It is somewhat smaller than a small egg. So for now we continue to dodge that bullet.

Battle Plan (Roger)

The next couple of entries are focused on the upcoming battle. This also is not surprising: Beginning in the late 1960's, Bruce received both textbook training and on the job training as to how to prepare for battle while in Vietnam. When he transitioned to the army service stateside in the National Guard, battle planning continued to be a priority for Bruce. Although the country was enjoying a period of peace, the constant threats to the country required that all armed services, including the National Guard, be prepared for any type of threat. This planning was a core competency that Bruce applied to all of his life: work at the Illinois State Police, his volunteering at church, and eventually his battle with cancer.

The information in the next couple of entries is included to provide assistance to those dealing with cancer, specifically prostate cancer. The resources where Bruce pulled his information are referenced in his journal in the following entries. He listed them in order to provide a head start for others that are beginning to start on the journey through prostate cancer. (Disclaimer Reminder: Neither Bruce nor I are medical professionals. The following is presented for informational purposes only. Refer to your medical professional with any questions.)

October 30, 2009 (Bruce)

Just finished reading the book "How We Survived Prostrate Cancer" by Victoria Hallerman. While waiting to see the doctor at the medical facility they had a newsletter which talked about prostrate cancer and mentioned the book. So I bought it. The book really resonated and I think it will be very helpful to me in the coming weeks and months.

Written Word (Roger)

Dad was a voracious reader. His collection of books started at a young age and continued throughout his life. The shelves in his den were always filled with books of all types: fiction, military history, how-to guides, biographies, books on all areas of history, and of course books on religion and theology. There were so many books that he would build new book shelves whenever he moved. And then fill those shelves with more books.

In his later years, his obsession with the printed word continued and started to manifest itself in Dad's Christmas gift list. The answer to the question of "What do you want for Christmas?" became "I made a list of books that I want to read". This presented an organizational obstacle for us because we had to coordinate the purchases from the list to ensure that we didn't purchase the same book from the list. To this day I can still remember many of the books that he asked for on his last Christmas list.

The previous journal entry is a perfect example: of course Dad would seek out books written by others that had gone through similar situations as to those he was facing. He was fortunate to find quite a few books that provided a high level of value through information, suggestions, and advice that aided his journey.

There were three books in particular that provided such a high level of value that he copied text directly from those books into his journal. These books are:

1. *"How We Survived Prostate Cancer"* by Victoria Hallerman - Dad was drawn to this book because it was a written account of a husband & wife's journey through the prostate cancer struggle. Dad realized that the journey that the Hallerman's went through was going to be similar to the journey that he and Mom would undergo as Dad fought prostate cancer. Dad found this book to be extremely insightful and recorded 26 key points from the book that were instrumental to him successfully overcoming prostate cancer. If you are facing prostate cancer, this book is an important one to purchase and read.

2. *"Guide to Surviving Prostate Cancer"* by Janet Farrar Worthington and Patrick C. Walsh - This was another important book that specifically provided insight and information as to improve the probability of conquering prostate cancer. In his journal, Dad focused on the health advice that was supplied in this book and recorded 16 specific improvements that he needed to make to his diet. This is another important book to purchase and read if you are fighting prostate cancer.

3. *"The Ragamuffin Gospel"* by Brennan Manning - The final book recorded in his journal, Dad relied upon this book for comfort, but not in the physical sense while he was fighting prostate cancer. Serious, potentially life-altering illnesses and situations shake our foundations, including our foundations of faith. Dad was not immune to this condition and found his faith challenged throughout his journey. This book was important to Dad's journey because the tools provided by Mr. Manning strengthened Dad's faith. After reading this book and taking the writing to heart, Dad found himself closer to God and more in tune with his mission for his remaining time on earth. This book played a key role in Dad's desire to help improve the lives of others.

These entries in Bruce's journal have been scrubbed from this writing because he literally copied the exact same words as found in the books; printing his journal as he wrote it would thus violate copyright law. However, it is important to include the lessons of these books in this writing because all three of them contain powerful insight, information, and advice for those going through struggles.

The important takeaway is that the books above would be beneficial to people going through conditions similar to those that Dad faced.

November 2, 2009 (Bruce)

I have been doing research on dietary modifications. The following items seem important; more can be found in Dr. Patrick Walsh's "Guide to Surviving Prostate Cancer."

Successes & Failures (Roger)

Dad included 16 dietary suggestions in the above journal entry that were pulled from this book. Every single one of these suggestions are common sense principles that we have learned all of our life. The advice includes such standard suggestions as eat your vegetables, reduce red meat consumption, all things in moderation, reduce grains, and, of course, a reminder to eat your vegetables.

However, despite his good intentions, for the most part, the dietary suggestions that Bruce wrote in his journal didn't stick. Dad continued to embrace a less than healthy diet for the rest of his years. Even though he was moderately active throughout the day, working around the house, going for walks with Mom, and biking every day, the weight never fell off significantly. His habit of having a bowl of ice cream or cereal at night before bed was just too strong to overcome. But it wasn't all necessarily his fault though: Coming from a Dutch background, there was a strong affinity for bread that we all swear is in our DNA.

It is reasonable to believe that Dad included this section in his journal to provide information to others going through a similar struggle. But there is another key to success found in this section as well: Dad wasn't perfect and his path to fighting prostate cancer wasn't without a misstep. Did he want to follow the advice in this book? Of course. But on the other hand, eating a steak was to Dad a glimpse of heaven. Not to mention his fondness for hamburgers.

Ultimately, the takeaway of this section is that it is OK to take a break or have an occasional stumble. The vast majority of us will experience periods of setbacks, whether those are self-inflicted or as a result of the disease. As long as forward progress is being made on a regular basis, the patient is fighting the good fight. The old saying is tried and true: "Two steps forward but one step forward" is still progress towards the goal.

As for you, the reader, as has been mentioned repeatedly in this book, consult your doctor to discuss whether modifications should be made to your diet.

November 10, 2009 (Bruce)

Traveling to Pueblo, Colorado, I received a phone call from the doctor advising me that the biopsy I had on my nose on November 3, 2009, was positive for basal cell cancer. I am to follow up in three months for another visit to the Dr to see if I am still having problems or did the biopsy get it all.

November 13, 2009

Received a phone call at 1:45p from the doctor's nurse that my prostate biopsy done on November 5, 2009 was positive for cancer. One sample was found to contain cancer and the Gleason score was 7. We were in the car with Marv (brother) and Jean (sister-in-law) and returning to their house after visiting mom and lunch. I have a follow up appointment on November 19th. I was not surprised as they had found PIN on the biopsy done in June. Nevertheless it was still a numbing experience. Donna asked how I felt and I said like crap. Later that day Donna called Don (brother-in-law) and Mary Lou (sister-in-law), and a few close friends. I called Jamie (son) and Roger (son). Wasn't easy. Later Jamie called about another issue and asked how I was and I said "good." He said, "No you're not."

Everyone in the car was silent. No one talked about it much; it is as if you don't talk about it maybe it's not true, however, I suspect no one knows exactly what to say. However, I had a desire to talk about it but that "gulf" was present. Maybe it would have been different if it had been only Donna and me.

Jamie and Roger asked a lot of questions and you could hear the concern in their voices. It was good to talk about it; no sense ignoring it as it is a reality and must be dealt with no matter how unpleasant the process will be.

Communicate (Roger)

All of us have different communication styles: Some want to talk about everything, some don't want to talk about anything, and there are a myriad of other types of styles in between those extremes. This is common knowledge as is the exhortation that people need to understand and appreciate the communication styles of the other people in the relationship. This understanding will improve the mechanics of the relationship. This is also true for those in the support network of the person going through struggles.

Consider the following thoughts from Bruce's previous journal entry:

"Everyone in the car was silent. No one talked about it much....However I had a desire to talk about it..."

The majority of this book uses positive examples from Bruce's journey to help others in similar situations Thrive during the struggle. This particular issue is the opposite however: Bruce and those in the car with him during the news from the phone call did not demonstrate productive communication. And in large part, this should have started with Bruce. It could have been a simple question: "Is it OK if we talk about it?" Of course the same question could have been posed to Bruce as well.

This is the reason it is important to have open conversations. Instead of talking about the situation, the struggles that Bruce was going through, or how the people in the car could assist Bruce, it was a quiet car ride. Ultimately, a period of time that could have been used for support, empathy, and edification, was absent all of these items that are necessary while in the midst of a struggle. Would the communication in the car have eliminated the struggle against a powerful disease? Probably not. But, at the very least, it could have helped ease the suffering during the journey.

Looking back, I am sure that Bruce would have agreed with the following advice:

- Don't be quiet.
- Don't assume that everyone knows what you are thinking.
- Do break the silence.
- Don't hide your feelings around those who love you.
- Finally: Don't be quiet.

November 15, 2009 (Bruce)

Went to see friends this morning after seeing mom. The couple were at Austin, TX, last year and had recently moved to Pueblo. They were very interested in my prostate experience as the husband had been dealing with a rising PSA and had a biopsy over a year ago. His was around 6.0 now but the Dr. had not said anything about another biopsy plus it had been awhile since the last PSA test. I mentioned that I thought he should pursue another PSA.

The wife later told Donna that she hoped our discussion had put a fire into the husband to do something. Some people seem to keep it "hush-hush" about prostate cancer but to me it should be out in the open. Maybe then people would not be so hesitant about having a PSA and biopsy done in the future. Maybe I was meant to be at these friends today so that he would pursue the issue. If nothing else this trip was made at this time for that reason.

November 18, 2009

Asked Roger to see what he could find out about the doctor with his soccer Dr. friends. He did and got back an email which said he was very good. That is a relief and substantiates what others seem to think about this doctor.

November 19, 2009

Saw the doctor today. My Gleason score of 7 was a 3-4 which is better than a 4-3. The doctor only does radiation seeds and I said my instinct is to have it out. The doctor said always go with your instinct. The doctor seems to favor robotics over the radical prostatectomy. After listening I concurred and an appointment was set up for Monday Nov 23rd at 7:15am with another doctor that does the robotics. I felt good about the conversation with the prostate doctor as the doctor

49

pretty much duplicated what I had been reading in Dr. Patrick Walsh's book "A Guide to Surviving Prostate Cancer."

In the book, which is very detailed, he raises questions about what you should ask your Dr. and how much experience the doctor should have. The stage was T1c which may or may not be significant. By having the prostate removed there will be further work done to see just how much cancer was in the prostate. With radiation this would not be possible. The doctor also thought that the lymph nodes would be removed. The doctor also indicated they do nerve sparing technique. This will help on the impotency/incontinence issue if nerves can be left behind. The prostate doctor also thought that the other doctor had probably done 300-400 of these surgeries.

Asked Roger to check out the new doctor with his friends. Later Roger received an email back from his contact saying that the new doctor was excellent.

Seek Support (Roger)

Bruce and Donna attended a support group at the local medical facility that was intended for patients and their spouses. There were approximately 10-15 people total which included spouses. The format was a standard classroom setup with a podium in the front and then rows of chairs for the audience. The leader would alternate between presenting information and conducting Q&A sessions. One of the meetings that made the largest impact was a session on taking care of the prostate through proper nutrition.

The offering was a limited time so Bruce and Donna were only able to attend a couple of sessions before they escaped the cold Illinois winter by spending time in Florida. When they returned to Illinois, the session was over. They didn't look for other support groups.

Read that sentence again: *"They didn't look for other support groups"*.

No one is perfect, especially when presented with a potentially life-ending disease. The stumbling through the disease is also greatly magnified for those facing diseases for the first time. Despite never having faced a particular disease, we often feel that we can handle it on our own. This urge to handle serious struggles on our own seems ingrained into our DNA. We must resist this urge and seek support from others.

If Bruce had to go through the circumstance again, he likely would have sought out more support groups. It is quite possible that there just weren't that many options available that focused on prostate cancer at that time. For all of Bruce's Internet sleuthing, there is no mention in his journals that he came across virtual online support groups.

Support is vital to the concept of thriving, both from the patient (and family) that is going through a disease and for the patient (and family) that have successfully battled the disease. It is a learning process for both groups that is extremely important in the healing process.

Are you going through a battle? Have you looked for groups, whether local or online, that could provide healing and support as you go through the struggle? It's worth the time and effort.

November 21, 2009 (Bruce)

Talked to a friend this morning and he was going to contact his daughter about the new doctor. Later got email that said "My daughter said the new doctor is really good with an excellent reputation."

Also called another friend this morning to discuss about the options and what I found out last Thursday. This friend was just about to call me. He called when we were in Cripple Creek, CO, to inquire. Nice to have these calls.

One of our previous ministers also called and left a message that if I wanted to talk to him to call. I did and found out that he had the seeds and he was very impressed with the staff at the medical facility. He has dealt with several of the doctors, although he did not know the new doctor. Possibly because of the treatment option he took.

It is interesting to see who contacts you when they find out about the cancer. So far I have had contacts from people who say that they are praying from people outside of the church, as well as a couple of ladies we worked with last year at the Springfield Overflow Shelter for the homeless.

Connecting (Roger)

Words matter.

A national news media outlet recently described the results of a statewide, off-cycle election as "devastating". This is curious because the generally-held description of the word devastating is something akin to Webster's definition as "causing great damage or harm". The example is "A devastating coastal tsunami could result from a severe displacement of the San Andreas Fault". Words matter and it seems like using the word "devastating" to describe the results of a democratic election might be a tad bit overreach.

Words matter. With the exception of the news media, this is a statement that everyone understands because we know that the rhyme we heard in elementary school is not accurate: "sticks and stones will break my bones, but words will never hurt me".

Despite inherently knowing that words matter, the vast majority of us get tripped up when it comes to knowing the right things to say to people that are going through trials and tribulations. We want to say something that will help them, to provide encouragement, but we are so concerned about saying the wrong thing that we usually only share a word or two with that person. The person that we care for deeply, the person going through a struggle, regardless of the specific stage of their struggle, this same person could use our encouragement.

Words matter. They help us connect with the person going through the struggle. This connection is important for many reasons:

- Provides encouragement to the person in the struggle (ie: the "patient") that others are thinking well of them and praying for their situation.
- Provides the baseline for a safe place for the patient to discuss their feelings about their struggle: their fears, their worries, their outlook on life.
- Outlines the specific situations that the friend or family member can lift up in prayer for the patient.
- Provides an outlet for the patient to vent about their situation.

As the date of the surgery neared, Bruce was conflicted as per the level of attention he did or did not receive from friends and family regarding the surgery. On the one hand he desired more contact, support, and prayer from his friends but on the other hand he didn't necessarily broadcast his feelings to his friends. He needed connection. But how were they to know what Bruce was needing?

Everyone is different and therefore connection requirements are different: One person might want to just hear from family and close friends. Others might want to hear from as many people as possible. Some might just want to hear that people are thinking and praying for their situation. Some might want to openly discuss their situation with as many people as possible.

The point is that there is no set formula that works with every person.

It would be of great benefit to all parties if the person going through the battle would recognize the level of communication that all parties in the relationship require during the journey. One fool-proof manner to establish this baseline is to engage in clear and open communication with family and friends. This communication will not be a one-time event because the needs of both the patient and the support network could change throughout the course of the struggle.

Open, clear, and direct communication is required between all parties in order to maximize the healing process.

December 15, 2009 (Bruce)

As time approaches my surgery date, more and more people are making contact. People from within and outside of the church. This includes not only the church in Springfield but also the church in Oregon, IL.

Last night at the elder's meeting, the elders after the meeting laid hands on me and prayed for healing and that the surgery goes well. This was a very moving moment and one in which it teaches a great deal about humility and concern that others have for you.

Today, a cousin called after she had heard about my cancer from Marv. Have not talked to her in a long time.

Tomorrow starts the day of a liquid diet prior to my surgery. Obviously not looking forward to that either.

Also received a call from another cousin who lived in Michigan. He had prostate surgery in Feb 2009 and is doing fine. He called to offer encouragement.

Gap in the Dates (Roger)

There is quite a bit of time between the last two journal entries as Bruce geared up for the life-changing surgery. His research was done. The selection was made. His mind was made up. Now all he had to do was wait for the surgery, which would have not been entirely new to him after his military career. There were many times throughout his life when he referenced the military's never-ending mantra of "Hurry Up and Wait".

What an agonizing month that must have been: four weeks, 28-30 days of waiting, imagining the worst possible outcomes. Well maybe Bruce was different and he suppressed thinking about the worst and instead focused on being able to move past the cancer and get on with his life.

The following is one of Bruce's writings that seems to be relevant for this period. Although it is dated many years before, it is likely to have been something that Bruce referred to often as he prepared to have his prostate removed.

"A Prayer of Despair and Faith" (Bruce)

<u>*Hebrews 12:2-3 (Berean Study Bible)*</u>

"Let us fix our eyes on Jesus, the author and perfecter of our faith, who for the joy set before him, endured the cross, scorning it shame, and sat down at the right hand of the throne of God. Consider him who endured such opposition from sinful men, so that you will not grow weary and lose heart."

<u>*James 1:3-4 (NIV)*</u>

"Consider it pure joy, my brothers, whenever you face trials of many kinds, because you know that the testing of your faith develops perseverance. Perseverance must finish its work so that you may be mature and complete, not lacking anything."

"LORD", I SAID:
   "I woke up and found myself
      floating in a fog.
   I had no feeling,
      but yet I could sense pain.
   Reality was here,
      but yet it wasn't.
   Time stood still,
      but events continued on.
   My mind understood,
      but my heart did not."

AND THE LORD SAID, "MY CHILD, HAVE FAITH"

I REPLIED:
   "Faith I have,
      but now the mesh appears too large.
   Like sand on a sieve,
      the grains are falling through.
   I wish they would stop,
      but I seem powerless to act.
   Like the draw of a black hole,
      I gravitate to the center,
   Immobile, lethargic and transfixed
      on a distant star."

AND THE LORD SAID, "MY CHILD, I UNDERSTAND"

I REPLIED:
   "I know that you do,
      but it's hard to understand.
   The trials and struggles
      that seem to have no end.
   The anguish and uncertainty
      just seem to wear me down.

At times it would be easy to say
   'I've had enough!'
But what purpose would that serve,
   and selfish wouldn't it be?"

AND THE LORD SAID, "MY CHILD, DON'T LOSE YOUR FAITH"

I REPLIED:
   "I know it's not for naught,
      if hope I do not lose.
   But alone I cannot stand,
      so I am yours to use.
   Take me in your arms,
      and carry me though this time.
   Restore in me the hope and faith
      that I once knew,
   So that once again together,
      we can do as you chose.

AND THE LORD SAID, "MY CHILD, TRUST ME, AND I WILL ALWAYS BE THERE"

AND I REPLIED:
   "Trust I will;
      forgive me when I falter.
   Give me strength,
      a hope renewed.
   Refine and hone me,
      sharper then before.
   Answers will need to wait,
      patience I must have,
   All will become clearer,
      when that final day is here."

AND THE LORD SAID, "MY CHILD, I AM HERE"

Whenever we feel like our trials and difficulties are never going to end, let us not lose heart. Let us even more fervently fix our eyes on our Lord and Savior and trust Him to be there for us. Let us not lose faith but instead persevere to the end.

Bruce W. VanderKolk (22 October 1994)

_____

Treatment

Public Service Announcement (Roger)

The prostate is out. The surgery to separate Bruce from the tiny organ called the prostate occurred on December 17, 2009. The recovery from the surgery lasted a few days in the medical facility and then several days passed while he recovered at home. (This explains the gap in his writings between the 15th and 31st of December.) He was back at writing as soon as he was physically and mentally able after surgery.

It is clear that a change has occurred in Bruce's journal. A new purpose arose in his life: to document his experiences after prostate cancer surgery with the goal of sharing with others as they went through a similar battle.

During the lead-up to the surgery, Bruce was surprised to find that he was not the only one dealing with prostate cancer amongst his friends and acquaintances. He leaned on them for advice, just as he wanted to be open to those who were in the same battle after he beat the cancer.

Bruce's discovery of these friends tied into the reality of the disease that it was a common cancer. The American Cancer Society estimates on prostate cancer confirms this:

- Other than skin cancer, prostate cancer is the most common cancer in American men
- In 2021 there were approximately 250,000 new cases of prostate cancer
- In 2021 there were approximately 34,000 deaths from prostate cancer
- About 1 man in 8 will be diagnosed with prostate cancer during his lifetime (13%)
- About 1 man in 41 will die of prostate cancer

But. But. The statistics are not all bad: More than 3.1 million men in the US who have been diagnosed with prostate cancer at some point are still alive today.

The surgery would also mark a major milestone in Bruce's life as he learned to deal with changes to the body in which he had dwelt for 64 years. As the journal continues, his experiences are described to help others walk through the valley more successfully than Bruce.

December 31, 2009 (Bruce)

Surgery is over, the year is coming to an end, and I look forward to 2010.

I saw the doctor this morning: There was no evidence that the cancer had gone outside of the prostate. No evidence of it in the lymph nodes, nerves or vascular area. This was all good news. The rating of the cancer had not changed and was still a 3 +4 for 7 Gleason Score. This was same as biopsy. There was an area that the cancer had spread to about 1mm from the edge which we knew from biopsy. That is one reason I decided to have it out as opposed to radiation. The spot on my bladder was also negative (during surgery they saw a white spot on the bladder and did a biopsy); I go back in a month for a follow-up PSA test. That will tell us a lot.

Last Monday I had the catheter removed and that was a major step forward. Since then I have been dealing with the issue of incontinence but it is better today than Monday. No problem when I sleep or sit but some problems when I get up or walk, move a certain way, or exert pressure.

Still having problems sleeping on either my left or right side. Must sleep most of the time on my back. I had six incisions but the one most troubling is the drainage tube incision which is on the right side of my stomach. It still has not totally healed over and I must change the bandage every day.

The surgery was about 3-3 1/2 hours with 2 hours in recovery. I spent one night in the medical facility which is good. I did do some walking at Roger's house with the catheter (around his living room and kitchen-65 feet each trip). This helped me get some of my strength back. Lost 5 pounds; now I need to keep it off.

I have had a lot of phone calls, visits in the medical facility, cards, and emails about getting well and how I am doing. These have been appreciated. I have kept these and list of those who called and visited. Not sure why but maybe it will be a reminder of what I should do for others.

During my recovery I have been reading a book received from Roger at Christmas called "The Ragmuffin Gospel", written by Brennan Manning. Very timely reading and seems to be appropriate for me at this time as I go through the prostate cancer process and recovery because the book speaks to how our faith grows during times of crisis.

As I reflect on various statements in the book about the reality of death, I find that there have been two defining moments in my life where I have had to come to grips with the potential of death. The first was Vietnam. Vietnam was a life-changing experience and I believe strongly that the 2LT who went to Vietnam was not the 1LT that returned. I faced death and became at peace that if God wanted me to survive and had other plans for me then that is what would take place. The prostate cancer is the second time. Again, it is all in His hands; there is nothing I can do which will alter the outcome (other than I should follow the advice of my doctors-again God's hand is in this). My question now is what I can do with God's help to make this a positive experience for me and others.

The Believer's Dichotomy (Roger)

Dad found the book "The Ragamuffin Gospel" to be so powerful that he again included direct quotes from the book into his journal. He included six quotes from the book that he felt spoke specifically to him as he was walking the thin line between life and death.

The broad takeaway from these quotations speaks to the level of hope that the believer in Jesus has when faced with the prospect that life on this earth is not eternal.

There is a dichotomy for the believer in the midst of this struggle. On the one hand, the believer is able to take comfort and solace in the fact that no matter what happens at the end of the struggle on the earth, the believer knows that eternity is on the other side. But on the other hand, that knowledge comes with the burden of wanting as many people as possible to be able to experience the eternal reality as well.

This was likely the mindset of Bruce during this journal entry as he recognized that his faith would grant him eternal life if his struggle was unsuccessful. But he didn't want to give up because he wanted to do what he could to enable others to experience this reality as well.

January 28, 2010 (Bruce)

It has now been six weeks since I had my surgery. At the time of my surgery six weeks seemed to be a long way off but now looking back it does not seem like six weeks have already gone by. I would say that I am progressing as well as expected according to what I have read. The pain around my stomach is pretty much gone. About a week and a half ago I overdid it on the treadmill by doing 3 miles at a 5.5% incline and 2.9 miles per hour and then followed it up with 3 miles at the mall. It took a week for the increased pain to get back to normal. I am just now doing a mile on the treadmill at 3.5% incline and 2.6 miles per hour. I have been walking 3 miles at the mall.

Other issues continue to be somewhat bothersome such as the incontinence; however, I believe that is also getting better. Tonight will mark a major breakthrough as I will not wear a pad to bed! The morning is not as bad as the later part of the afternoon. It also is based upon not drinking to excess, watching how I move and being careful not to put too much stress on my lower abdomen.

This past Monday I had blood drawn for PSA test and will see the doctor on Monday, Feb 1, 2010, for the results. This will tell how successful the surgery was and whether or not I still have a potential problem.

I feel good about the surgery and have not been "down" about some of the issues mentioned above. I intend to ask the doctor if I can start doing the recumbent bike and how long before I can ride a regular bike.

People have been great and have shown concern and still ask how I am doing. I appreciate that and would rather discuss the issue as opposed to not talking about it.

I purchased four wrist bands that alternated blue and pink colors and both Donna and I wear this as she had breast cancer and I had prostate cancer. I have also been wearing the prostate bracelet. Today I gave a prostate ribbon and bracelet to my neighbor and intend to give same to a dear friend.

Brotherhood (Roger)

In 2004, people began wearing yellow silicone bracelets with the word "Livestrong" molded into the bracelet. The bracelets were developed as a fund-raising effort for Lance Armstrong's Livestrong foundation to increase funding for research aimed at eliminating cancer. Regardless of how you feel about Lance Armstrong, there is no denying that his efforts brought cancer research to the forefront of the collective consciousness and brought millions of dollars to that research. It is estimated that over $500 million has been generated.

The yellow bands provided a visible sign to people that either the person was going through cancer, had gone through cancer, knew someone with cancer, or was contributing to the fight to end cancer.

Bruce felt drawn to these bracelets: He purchased a yellow Livestrong band well before he started his battles with cancer.

When he started the battle against prostate cancer, he did a lot of online research to find a specific band for prostate cancer because they were not readily available at that time. When he found a suitable bracelet for prostate cancer, he purchased several bracelets. Bruce wore the bracelet everywhere: In the home, out while running errands, while exercising, while sleeping, even while showering.

He wore the bracelet because he wanted to let people know that he had prostate cancer. He wanted to use it to generate conversations with those going through the disease or conversations with those who had successfully fought the disease. He specifically felt an urge to have conversations with those recently diagnosed with prostate cancer.

He also found bracelets with two colors that communicated a battle with two types of cancer. He purchased bracelets that were linked to prostate and breast cancers to empathize with Donna who had battled breast cancer in 1989.

Bruce used the bracelets as a tool to build connections.

If you are going through similar struggles, what are you using to build connections? It may be silicon bracelets. It may be stickers on your back bumper. It may be something else new that wasn't around while Bruce was in the midst of his battles. The type of tool isn't necessarily important. What is important is building connections.

If you're a friend or family member of someone going through battles, what tools are you using to build connection?

February 1, 2010 (Bruce)

Thank you God! I met with the doctor today and my PSA reading was less than 0.008 or basically "0". That is great news. If it stays at that level it means that the cancer is gone. This was a welcome relief and best news in a long time. I also asked if the cancer had spread beyond the original biopsy location and the doctor said it was in both the left and right area and also covered about 20% of the prostate. That is also good news as the average number of areas found after removal is around 7 different areas if found in one biopsy area. I also have no further restrictions, e.g. I can lift, bike, do pushups, sit-ups, and whatever I want to do. I will start doing the recumbent inside bike and some pushups and sit-ups but not a lot.

June 17, 2010

It has now been six months since my surgery. I feel good and my two PSA tests I have had since then were: Jan 25, 2010 less than 0.008 and May 4, 2010 less than 0.008. As the doctor said it is at zero. I do not have any lasting effects except I am still dealing with the issue of minor incontinence which requires the use of a small pad. This incontinence is stress (pressure) related, e.g. the more strenuous the activity and type of pressure on the lower stomach will determine if there will be leakage and the amount of leakage. The doctor does not seem too concerned at this point. I have read that this may take a year to clear up. The issue of sexual function is in about the same level of recovery.

I have noticed that it is harder to lose weight as I have put on additional pounds; however, I am also not exercising well because of the incontinence. The only other change I have noticed is that my blood pressure seems to be running about 10 points higher on both the upper and lower numbers. I was on a prescription for a certain drug but had several side effects and quit taking the drug after discussion with the doctor.

From a "mind-set" mode I cannot get the aspect of my having cancer and the potential of it returning out of my mind. It is there daily and in many respects resembles the constant recurring memories of Vietnam which never seem to leave you alone. Sometimes I wonder if I'm not just a bit off the bubble. I know my attitude is not the same and I am not sure I take the pressures of life as easily as I did before. In many respects the expression of "joy" has been chipped away and I am more serious than before. I also seem to have an incessant drive to be busy and in a hurry to get things done as if "time" is running out. Maybe it is. Having recently inherited money we are debt free. Coincidence or God driven is the question as these two aspects work together. Only time will tell.

August 17, 2010

Saturday I took a large step forward and decided to try working around home etc. without wearing the incontinence pad (I have been down to only one a day for several weeks). Well today marks the 4th day and everything has been OK-no accidents. This was actually a major step in that it took confidence to try going without the "support" factor. I am more aware of watching certain movements but I am sure with time that awareness will become automatic and I am no longer aware of what is taking place. Thursday will mark the 35th week since I had surgery.

This past Sunday I also spoke to an individual manning a booth at the IL State Fair from the IL Dept of Veterans' Affairs about prostate cancer and disability pay. This person said without question I should file for disability because of the potential benefits. They also said you can continue to see whatever Dr. you want to see-you do not need to see a VA doctor. They gave me the contact and I need to check this out.

September 7, 2010

The good news is that I do not have the need to wear the incontinence pads. One step forward! However, there is also at least one step backwards. For several weeks I have been experiencing pain in my stomach and it seems like the belly button was extended and an area above was harder and protruding. I thought maybe I had strained a stomach muscle but it continued to get more intense so I went to see the doctor on August 30th. The doctor wasn't sure what the problem was but did notice it and was able to work me in to see the doctor that removed the prostate the next day. This doctor said I have a Ventral Hernia (an incision hernia). The doctor walked up stairs and was able to have another doctor perform an examination and confirmed the Ventral Hernia and said the only solution was surgery and to have a mesh inserted to repair the problem. I was able to immediately get the pre-op done and am scheduled for September 9th. This was the first available opening. Really quick process.

Needless to say I have gone through the cycle of being angry, feeling sorry for myself and the swings of highs and lows. I am also more apprehensive about this surgery than the prostate surgery in December. Maybe because I had anticipated for months that I would end up with prostate cancer as my PSA kept rising. This came very unexpectedly and with no time to mentally prepare for the news.

I had the staff devotions today and read a short article sent by a friend in *church to me a few weeks ago about how God closes doors because He has other plans. Many times we keep trying to open the closed door instead of accepting that God wants me to take a different path. The closed door this time means our trip to Mackinaw Island is off and also my return to a bike exercise routine. I consider these doors closed but do not know why or what door I am to walk through now.*

September 12, 2010

Well, the surgery was September 9, 2010, at 6:55a at the local medical facility. Dr came out after the surgery to talk to Donna and indicated it went well. However, I had a difficult time dealing with the pain in recovery and received a couple of additional doses of pain killer. I could not sit up without a lot of pain. Eventually I did but then had a difficult time not getting dizzy-had to lie back down. Finally, was able to stand and was released. There has been a lot more pain than I anticipated and am still sleeping in the recliner as I cannot raise myself up without the use of pulling on something. Tried the bed last night but it did not work. Still cannot lie on my side (either one). Spend a lot of time sleeping during the day. Try to walk around some but it is difficult. Went off the pain killer yesterday and started to take over-the-counter medicine instead. Counted 9 incisions of varying size around my stomach. Some of the skin came off when I removed some of the larger bandages-strips had to stay on. These areas are also painful. Someone told Donna at church today that the reason for this is because I had an allergic reaction to the plastic bandages.

Anchors (Roger)

The oscillating cycles have returned and they have returned with a vengeance:

- The cycle between Hope and Despair
- The cycle between Life and Death
- The cycle between Living and Giving In
- The cycle between Being Grateful for Life and Anger

Bruce wasn't unique when he experienced these cycles. We all do to some extent. It is simply a fact of life. Sometimes things are good.

Sometimes things are not so good.

When faced with a potentially life-ending disease, these cycles are amplified of course. The highs are higher while the lows are extremely low.

Perhaps Bruce was right when he described these waves of feelings as oscillating cycles. When people navigate through these waves in everyday life, it is akin to a normal electric pattern: small, predictable, evenly-spaced waves. But the pattern changes when faced with life altering situations: the waves become greater, less predictable, and the low periods are significantly longer than the high periods.

But perhaps there is another way to think of these periods: ocean waves. In 2017, Bruce and Donna moved full time to southwest Florida where they were able to spend time on the open water of large bays and the Gulf of Mexico. They didn't spend a lot of time on the water, but the time that they did spend was usually filled with the ups and downs of the waves, whether it was from the large waves of the Gulf or smaller waves in the bay that were created by passing larger fishing boats. Bruce quickly came to appreciate the power of boat anchors to stabilize the craft and lessen the waves' impact on the boat.

Anchors. Boats need them, but I would postulate that we need them also because we all experience the ups and downs of waves as we go through life.

There are two songs in contemporary Christian music currently that focus on the importance of having the right anchor as we navigate the stormy waters of this life. One is by the group Skillet and the other is by Crowder. The lyrics of both are strong and powerful reminders of the importance of having a solid anchor in our lives. For Bruce and all Christians, this anchor is Christ. As is written in the book of Hebrews:

"We have this hope as an anchor for the soul, firm and secure..." (Hebrews 6:19, NIV)

Timing is everything in life. Unfortunately timing doesn't always work out the way we believe it should. The lyrics to Crowder's song specifically would have spoken directly to the struggle that Bruce was going through at this point in his life. Unfortunately the song was released in 2021, 3 years after Bruce's passing on to the next life.

But don't let that be your excuse. The lyrics are powerful and will speak to you, no matter the waves you are going through in life. Go online and read these lyrics, download the song, and let it minister to your situation.

November 8, 2010 (Bruce)

It has been two months since the hernia surgery and the recovery has taken longer than I anticipated. For several weeks I had pain in the upper left part of my abdomen. I mentioned it to a good friend from church and he prayed for healing. The next day that pain was gone and has been gone every since. I have had pain off and on in the lower left area. It even bothered me coming back to Illinois after we saw our old minister and his wife the end of October. In fact I was tempted to contact the doctor but then after a few days it was not as intense. It is better now and I will wait and see.

November 9, 2010

Saw the doctor today and my PSA results from last week were for all practical purposes zero. It was below the 0.008 mark and the doctor said below that it is impossible to get a reading. This is very good news as I am coming up on the one year mark. It does not mean I am cancer-free but that there is not any detectable prostate cancer. I also was a guinea pig today as the doctor had a new nurse practitioner today who never had done a digital exam on someone without a prostate. The doctor asked if it was ok for the practitioner to do it. What do you say in a situation like that except yes. The doctor did mention that this still needs to be done once a year in case there is a tumor that forms. I thought I was done with these tests and only needed to do the PSA. Oh well.

December 17, 2010

One year, still alive. Praise God.

December 28, 2010

Well, it just doesn't stop. Last week I noticed a bulge, large, in the center of my abdomen when I would exert pressure on the stomach, such as when doing a sit up. I compared it to a French loaf. I called the medical facility and the nurse suggested I have the doctor look at it. Well, it is another abnormality called "Diastases Rectus." It occurs when the vertical muscles in the abdomen decide to separate with half going to the right and half to the left. The center part is weak and therefore the bulge. The doctor said it is not related to the ventral hernia and that it is not uncommon. At this time there is nothing that needs to be done and the doctor said I have no restrictions. At some point it could become a hernia or some other associated problem. This certainly has been a long 12 months.

May 9, 2011

Saw the doctor today for my 1 ½ year check. The doctor reported that the PSA results were zero (actual report showed 0.008). Go back in 6 months, however, not sure if I need to see this doctor again or if I can see a Dr closer to home.

November 14, 2011

Saw the prostate doctor today for my 2 year check. PSA results the doctor said were zero (actual report showed 0.008). Praise the Lord. Go back in 6 months as the doctor wants to continue to check it every 6 months until I reach 5 years.

Helping Others (Roger)

At this point in time, it has been two years and five months since Bruce's life was changed with the prostate cancer diagnosis. As you've read, it was a time period that seemed like the world's longest roller-coaster with an infinite number of ups and downs. But through it all, Bruce was faithful to his calling of helping to improve the lives of others. No matter which church he was attending, he made it a point to serve on the missions committee to lend his assistance and expertise to the church's mission of improving the world. The Missions Committees were very important to Dad. Through his work on those mission committees, Bruce was able to thrive.

Bruce wrote the following in 2014, in the midst of a whole new set of medical issues. But it is important for this time frame because it speaks to his mindset of the importance of helping others.

Abba, Father (Bruce)

A member of Anchor Christian Church performed a new song that I had not heard before during a Wednesday night worship service on Feb 5, 2014. I did some research and discovered that the song was called "Abba, Father" by Hillsong Worship.

The lyrics really spoke to me: it is a moving song about how privileged we are to be saved by grace and the love we have for our Father.

But this song also tells another message; a message about those who do not have the same privilege. It tells the story about:

Those who do not have the strong hand to guide us
Or a voice that soothes us
The absence of open arms
A void of worship
A precious Savior unknown
Lips that fail to praise
And an emptiness without hope.

As Christians, Christ has given us the mandate to spread the gospel. This is what "Missions" is all about. Through our Missions giving and personal witness, we can help someone else voice the words "Abba, Father how I love you."

Bruce VanderKolk (February 6, 2014)

Outward Focus (Roger)

As noted on the date, Bruce pulled together the previous writing in 2014, well after his battle with prostate cancer. But it seems appropriate for this period in his life because the message would have spoken to him during the early stages of the prostate cancer fight. Or all of our lives for that matter when we face struggles. Bruce wanted to convey that life is not ours to determine. A simple check of the news reports demonstrates that man is fallen and that this world is light years away from perfect. There is no such thing as an easy life. There is no such thing as a life that we can plan, dictate, or control.

No, ours is to live our lives in such a way to be a beacon of hope to others. As is written in the fifth book of Matthew:

"You are the light of the world. A town built on a hill cannot be hidden. Neither do people light a lamp and put it under a bowl. Instead they put it on its stand, and it gives light to everyone in the house. In the same way, let your light shine before others, that they may see your good deeds and glorify your Father in heaven." (Matthew 5:14-16, NIV).

The entries from Bruce's journals thus far in book occurred during the roughly two-year period from 2009-2011. There is no confusion about that period because it was filled with pain. He had both physical and mental pain, along with anguish, uncertainty, confusion, questioning, anger, grief, and quite likely some rebellion.

But through it all, Bruce pushed and endeavored to not only make his life an example for others but he actually worked to minister to others as well. He did not despondently sit in his recliner watching the television as the clock continued its ever movement into the future. Instead he got out of the chair as much as possible. Bruce didn't just survive, he **thrived!**

During that two year span, Bruce was involved in the following activities to help others:

- "Paid" position as Administrator at his church. 8 hours per day, 4 days per week Bruce worked to ensure that the entirety of the staff worked successfully together. The importance was to enable the church to more effectively accomplish its mission of ministering to everyone.
- Taught an adult Sunday School class weekly. The purpose was to facilitate discussion amongst the class to help others in their daily walk and to deepen their faith. I know what you're thinking: "Big deal. Who hasn't spent an hour a week teaching a Sunday school class?" Well, for Bruce it was different. He felt very strongly that if he was going to teach a class that he needed to be as prepared as possible prior to walking into the classroom. He spent many hours each week preparing for the class.

- Worked as Executive Minister during the period after the Senior Minister moved, fulfilling all the duties of the Senior Minister with the exception of the weekly preaching.
- Drove Strategic Planning effort at church to ensure that the church was positioned for long-term growth and ministry. The purpose was to ensure that the church was laser-focused on their mission. Laser-focused for the foreseeable future.
- Worked at Christian youth camp for two winters in Texas to improve the facilities. The purpose was to ensure that the camp was suitable for its mission of reaching others for Christ.

Bruce's goal was two-fold. First, to provide encouragement to others that life can get better. Second, to make his life an example for those going through similar life-altering circumstances. He showed, through his actions, that there is hope beyond the struggle.

That is the purpose of Thriving though, isn't it? "To grow or develop successfully; to flourish or succeed; to progress toward or realize a goal despite or because of circumstances."

_____

Intermission

The Importance of a Plan (Roger)

Thus far, we have followed two years of Bruce's journey through cancer and other medical issues. Now that he had "beaten" prostate cancer as evidenced by the organ's removal and the ultra-low PSA readings, Bruce would have expected to resume a "normal" life. But life had other plans. In other words, other severe medical issues presented themselves.

However, before we continue on with Bruce's journey, let's pause for a bit and focus on your journey.

None of us are on the same journey. Some of you might have recently received the life-changing news and face an uncertain future. Perhaps some of you are already well on your way to winning the battle and getting ready to claim the new normality of life. Many more of you are likely in the middle of your journey, beyond the starting point but still a distance from the end of your journey.

In the Diagnosis period of Bruce's journey, there was a section called "Battle Plan". I realize that the vast majority of the readers likely do not have military experience, but it was important to highlight this concept in how it helped Bruce navigate his struggles.

Planning was a way of life for Bruce. Whether he was working his day job with the State of Illinois, volunteering his evenings at the church, or working at the National Guard during his weekends, Bruce was planning. The importance of planning was likely most critical for his work with the National Guard. For one weekend a month, Bruce and the rest of his unit staff would be planning how to succeed in virtually any battle scenario. But that's not all: Bruce and his unit were also required to engage in a "summer camp" for two weeks. We always gave him a hard time that he was just going on vacation away from the family, sitting by the pool or at the campsite for those two weeks. We of course knew that summer camp was an important tool for the army because it allowed the soldiers to hone their craft by putting their plans to the test of action.

Bruce's final unit was a chemical brigade, where they were tasked with overcoming potential chemical, nuclear, and biological attacks by foreign entities. The time frame of his command was the 1990's, which was still a period of global unrest. It was vitally important for Bruce's unit to be fully prepared for every type of eventuality by having a fully vetted plan. Only with a solid, well-crafted plan would they be prepared to successfully defeat the enemy.

Right now you may be saying, "So what? Who cares? Big deal. How does this help me in my struggle?"

Anecdotal evidence that I have collected while writing this book suggest that the many people going through a serious medical struggle lack a defined plan. This complicates their struggle. The struggle is hard enough for everyone, even those with a plan. To not have a plan adds a level of difficulty to your struggle. It's an overused cliche, but it is true: You're in a battle and you need a plan.

The takeaway from this concept of battle planning is that you don't need to be military to begin this habit. Your battle plan is unique to you. It can be something as simple as a sticky-note on your bathroom mirror with a favorite scripture or word of encouragement. It could be as elaborate as a 50-slide presentation that describes the process from where you are at today to where you want to be on the other side of the battle.

It is key that you have a plan. Without a plan, the age-old saying is true: All you have is hope, and hope is not a strategy.

Have you started creating your battle plan?

Have you shared it with your brother/sisterhood?

Troughs, not Crests

Unfortunately, Bruce's story got worse before it got better. The prostate cancer had been dealt with and was no longer a concern. Sure, there were still checkups, but for the most part, the removal of the organ had created an atmosphere where the uncertainty and stress that the cancer could come back had been greatly diminished. That was the good news.

The bad news was that the thyroid issue came back, along with other health conditions, that make this particular period of time a very difficult set of circumstances for Bruce. Given everything that he had been through, from the Vietnam war to all of the health scares from 2009-2011, he could have deservedly been given a pass to curl up in a ball and remove himself from life.

This following chapter deals with those events and the struggles that Bruce found himself going through during this period. He would go through additional issues with his thyroid, a pretty major bicycle accident, a hernia, and a few instances of skin cancer.

But that is not what you will find as you read through this chapter. What you will discover are the writings and thoughts of a person who believed that even through the darkest of circumstances, three things are true:

1. God is Good.
2. All the time.
3. God will use us to accomplish His plan.

Despite going through many medical issues in the next 2-3 years, Bruce believed in the above truths and made the decision.

He decided to Thrive.

———————————————————

Beyond Prostate Cancer

December 15, 2011 (Bruce)

Saw the doctor today about the problem I am having with the pain in my side. Has been an issue since my ventral hernia operation in Sept 2010, however, seems to be getting worse. I had previous to the visit an ultrasound which showed "sludge" in my gall bladder; however the doctor did not think that was the problem. The doctor scheduled me for a CT on December 19. The doctor also stated that doing the previous hernia by laproscopy surgery was not a good option. This doctor does not do it that way and instead does a single incision to repair the hernia. Found out later by looking on the Internet at other hernia centers that they also do it the way that this doctor suggests. Not pleased again with the previous medical facility.

December 16, 2011

Woke up today and could not see out of my right eye except for some sight around the edges. It was like looking through a frosted windshield. Saw the doctor in the morning and was given some drops to put in my eye to see if that cleared the floaters away.

December 22, 2011

Saw another doctor today and found out the results of the CT. The doctor showed where I have another hernia in about the same position. The doctor is not sure if it is new or the previous repair did not get it. Will not know until the doctor operates which is the path the doctor feels should be done. However, the doctor said it was OK to go to Florida but do not do any heavy lifting.

December 28, 2011

Saw the doctor again about my eye. The doctor did not see any improvement and thought it was worse. The doctor said I should see a specialist as soon as possible. The doctor believes I have a vein occlusion which is a partial blocking of the vein carrying blood away from the eye. Told the doctor I was going to Florida which complicated the matter. Said we were going to southern Florida and the doctor knew some Drs in the vicinity and would set up an appointment. The doctor wanted me to go to across the state but that would not be good for Donna to drive.

January 10, 2012

Saw the doctor today and the appointment lasted about 2+ hours. Many tests and finally the doctor said I do have a vein occlusion. I have leaky veins and in the doctor's opinion this is caused by blood pressure. Another name for this is eye stroke. The doctor said there was a lot of swelling on the macular -I believe. The doctor recommended that I have shots in my eye using a drug which has been used for macular degeneration and was recently approved by the FDA for my type of eye problem. The doctor said I could start today so I did. This is not a pleasant process and for about 3 ½ hours afterwards it felt like I had sand in my eye. Next few days also had a slight headache above the eye. The doctor hit a vein in the white of my eye and for 5 days I had a blood colored right eye. Evidently all of this is not unusual although not everyone has these problems. There are also more severe problems with the drug such as stroke, heart attack etc. There are about 10 possible causes for this condition but the main three are blood pressure, diabetes, and glaucoma. My next shot is scheduled for Feb 7, 2012.

Mary Lou (sister in law) has been told her eye problem is also a vein occlusion. However, her injections are with a different drug. Additionally, she has lost vision only for a very short time, e.g. 15-30 minutes. Mine is now like a gray band across the center of my eye and it is not going away.

January 17, 2012

Saw the doctor again today for more tests, including looking into the eye. I did do better reading the letter charts today so there is some improvement. The doctor seemed satisfied with the progress although it has only been a week. There were no signs of infection which the doctor was concerned about. The doctor said the drug is still in the eye and will continue to work. Guess that is why you wait a month for the second shot. The doctor said it will take a couple more shots to see what happens. The doctor seems optimistic compared to what I read on the Internet.

February 7, 2012

Had my second shot in the eye today with an injection of the drug that was administered in January. This is not a very pleasant procedure and as last time the eye was sore for about 3 ½ hours. Tried drops in the eye but that did not help *much. Trying to keep the eye closed also did not help: I just must gut it out. The doctor seemed satisfied with the progress and the tests showed that the swelling had gone down a lot. However, I am beginning to think that I will never regain full vision in the eye. You just have to ask yourself the question why? Why must these things happen when everything seems to be going ok?*

I do have an appointment March 14, 2012 at a medical facility back home with another doctor. This doctor appears to be well-known. This is the same doctor Mary Lou (sister-in-law) sees.

Get out of Bed (Roger)

None of us is guaranteed a lifetime of sunshine, rainbows, and butterflies. There will be periods of time where the good times and bad times compete against each other, throwing our lives into turmoil.

At this point in time, Bruce must have been the equivalent of the grizzled old sea captain, the kind that is used to the ups and downs of the waves of the sea, and just plugs forward. It is now coming up to 4 years where Bruce has fought one battle after another, with no sustained periods of peace.

His perseverance was remarkable and was an inspiration for all of us, not just those going through cancer, serious illnesses, or other devastating life circumstances.

One may ask, "How did he do it?" How did he manage to wake up in the morning unsure of what bad news life was going to bring him that day? But more importantly for us: How can we do it? How can we wake up and get out of bed when we are in the troughs of the waves?

The first step is the most critical: Get out of bed. No, really. Physically, when you wake up in the morning, get out of the bed with the purpose to go about your day. Bruce and Donna made it a point to take life day by day as Bruce was going through this struggle. But the first step was to get out of bed.

Once out of bed, they went about their normal routines, whenever and however possible. Their minds were on their activities: chores around the house, church, going out to eat, putting puzzles together, playing games with family, etc. Bruce liked to putter in the garage working on projects. The activities were a welcome diversion from the reality of the struggle and kept their minds going in different directions. Forward direction, not a woe-is-us direction.

Bruce also no doubt took solace from Scripture as he navigated through the waves of his struggle. Previously we have pointed to the comparison of God being our anchor and relying on him for stability during times of struggle. One can also imagine that the story of Peter walking on water (Matthew 14) helped Bruce to focus on the long term picture: the struggles of this earthly life are nothing compared to the glory when we pass on to the next heavenly life.

The waves of life will never go away. At least not on this earth. The waves will be more severe for some people than others. But waves are constant: small, large, calm, or stormy. Bruce understood this. Even through the storms, like the apostle Peter, we can focus on Jesus and move forward in His hope of a time without turmoil.

March 8, 2012 (Bruce)

Saw the doctor today about my hernia as it seems to be getting worse. The doctor scheduled surgery for April 4, 2012, at a medical facility. Because of the prior surgery, the doctor was not sure what might be found and decided to do an open surgery as opposed to laparoscopic.

March 14, 2012

Saw a doctor and went through a battery of tests-similar to what I had with the doctor in Florida. This doctor thought the eye was looking good and now it is a question of maintenance. The doctor wants to continue the shots for a year but switched me from the previous drug to another one. The doctor said they both produce the same results except the new drug only costs $50 a shot versus $2000 for the old drug. The doctor did think I needed new glasses. For some reason when this doctor gave the shot it hurt more than when the doctor in Florida gave the shots. Bothered me going home and I slept-I am really beginning to hate these shots.

April 10, 2012

Well, had the surgery on April 4th and it appears all went well. The doctor did the open cut, approximately 4 inches, and repaired the prior mesh-appears it had partially come loose, and added another mesh about 1 x 4 inches. Did not need to stay overnight. Surgery was about 1 ½ hours starting around 10:45a. Been sleeping on the recliner again as it is sore and lying in bed just doesn't work. Did this for about 5 nights. We need to stop all of these surgeries. Cannot lift anything over 10 pounds for six weeks.

April 17, 2012

Saw the doctor today and the hernia was doing very well. Need to see this doctor again on the 8th of May. The doctor was surprised at how much activity I was doing (mowed lawn once). Talked to Marv (brother) and he compared me to the cartoon character who walks around with a cloud over his head and it is always raining.

April 30, 2012

Saw the doctor again today. Got my 4th shot in the eye, again it was the new drug. My vision was back to 20/300 but the pin wheel vision was around 20/50. The doctor thought I should be seeing better and suggested new glasses. Told the doctor I just got new glasses and the doctor suggested having them checked. I did mention to one of the student Drs who looked at me first that I did not think my vision was as good after the new drug as it was after the previous drug. The doctor did mention that my vision probably would not be improved but these shots were for maintenance. Found out later that the new drug is a chemo drug used to treat some types of cancer. It stops the formation of new blood vessels which seems odd to use as at the prior visit the doctor said the eye needed to start new blood vessels to work around the clot in the eye. I found out on the Internet that there is no method to remove the clot from the vein. The abbreviation for my situation is CRVO (central retinal vein occlusion). I am not as confident in this doctor as I was with the previous doctor. This doctor doesn't seem to me to like questions and the doctor provides very little information unless prompted. The doctor may be well known and has good credentials but the bedside manner is not what I need at this time.

May 7, 2012

Had my first visit with a new doctor. Also had another PSA test. The doctor said my PSA results were below the limit of detection or zero. This is good news after two and half years since my prostate removal.

Saw another doctor today at a medical facility. This was for an annual checkup on my thyroid. The doctor noticed that I had a large growth on the thyroid and possibly some of the lymph nodes were enlarged. As a result the doctor has scheduled me for an ultrasound of the thyroid on the 29th of May, 2012. Seems like we are back to where we were three years ago at about the same time of the year. The doctor discussed the possibility of doing a biopsy but later also discussed that surgery might be needed for this large of a growth. The doctor was also going to look to see what blood tests I have had recently as these can indicate problems with the thyroid.

That little rain cloud above my head just doesn't want to move away.

Personal Confession (Roger)

I get a lot of flack from a neighbor when I say that I have a dark rain cloud above me, following me around. He looks at me and responds with a question: "How many people are coming to your party?" To which I look at him like he is crazy and say "what party?" He responds: "Your pity party".

A little harsh? Perhaps. But it's exactly what I need to hear. His point is 100% valid: Each of us makes the choice when we wake up in the morning how we are going to approach the day. We can either choose to be negative (me) or choose to be positive and provide energy and encouragement for others (him).

I cannot imagine going through all of the battles that Dad was fighting. Nor can I imagine going through the battles that you are going through as you read these pages. But my neighbor's admonishment remains true to all: **Choose** how you respond to what life throws at you.

Dad had his prostate removed. He had issues with his thyroid. He fought through a couple of hernia surgeries. And now, Dad is fighting the potential for long term vision loss.

But Dad chose to thrive during all of these struggles. He of course doesn't mention it in the journal because he was humble and didn't want to come across as bragging or putting himself above others. Throughout this entire ordeal, amongst all the struggles, Dad continued to work to improve the lives of others. He continued to work at the church. He continued to volunteer for various ministry opportunities at the church. He continued fellowshipping with his friends. He reached out to those he knew that were going through times of struggle.

How many people were in Dad's pity party? Zero.

How many people are in yours?

May 22, 2012 (Bruce)

This represents a summary of what has occurred over the past few days and is being documented as it is the third time for such an event. On the 18th of May after working at Roger's house building some shelves, I had difficulty urinating. Starts ok but then it feels like a spasm is taking place which is extremely painful in the lower abdomen for about 5-10 seconds. Obviously I cannot totally empty the bladder and requires more frequent trips to the restroom. This continued until May 21 at which time in the afternoon it started to go away. This is the third time for this situation. The first was in 2010 after working with Jamie cutting wood in the summer-very hot day; the second was in 2011 also in the summer after I had biked 66 miles. I am not sure if it is a combination of exercise and dehydration or pressure on the nerves in the bladder area. In Nov 2011 I mentioned it to the doctor and the doctor seemed to imply it was the nerves as a result of sitting on the bike for an extended period of time. I never had anything like this prior to my prostate cancer operation in Dec of 2009. I believe there is some type of correlation. This time I also had diarrhea over the same period of time. The combination was debilitating.

I think the following quote is very appropriate from Job 14:1-2,

"Man born of woman is of a few days and full of trouble. He springs up like a flower and withers away. (NIV)"

I feel like I am in the withering stage of my life as one ailment follows another with increasing frequency. After so many years of good health and being able to do what I wanted to do this becomes difficult to cope with at times. I realize in my head that I should not let it affect me as whatever happens is for a reason and I should not be exempt. God is in control. Now that being said, in practical terms the emotions can take control over the logical thinking aspect of our being. It does cause one to think about life and what has gone before and what lies ahead. In retrospect and in terms of the world I have accomplished a lot. Not everyone can speak to being a Brigadier General and at the same time serve full time as the Commander of the Illinois State Police Forensic Science Command. But these things came at a cost; a cost to family and my contribution of service to mankind. At times I am not sure the two achievements are important or whether the cost was too high.

May 29, 2012

Today I had an ultrasound of my thyroid. It was obvious that the tech was finding things as I could see the tech mark areas showing height and width. Afterwards I was asked to wait while the tech showed the pictures to the Dr. to see if anything else needed to be done. This was unusual as I have not had that happen before. The tech said I should hear about the results in one or two days.

May 30, 2012

While working at Don's today building his screened-in-porch, I received a call in the early afternoon from the doctor who mentioned that I had several nodules (5-6), that were on both sides of the thyroid and they were in the 1.5 cm range in size. The large one in the center of the thyroid was 4.4cm (about 14 months ago the ultrasound showed this to be around 2.4cm). The doctor discussed the next course of events as being either a biopsy or surgery. I had the clear impression that because of the size and my history (radiation treatments as a teenager for acne) that surgery was a better choice. I told the doctor I would go for the surgery. The doctor said that was a good choice. I asked if the surgery could wait until after our trip to Colorado which would mean not earlier than the 10th of July. The doctor said that would probably be ok. (From my perspective, if I have cancer and it is the bad kind which is very aggressive and about a 1% chance of cure, waiting would not make any difference; on the other hand if I have cancer and it is the better type with over 90% survival waiting would not make a difference; same thing if it is not cancer.)

The doctor could suggest a surgeon or I could call another doctor and ask for a recommendation. I indicated I would follow the doctor's suggestion. The doctor gave me a name of a medical facility near here. I decided to call another medical facility to check references. They were aware of the Dr. and also mentioned the possibility of the doctor who did one of my other surgeries. It was unknown if this doctor did thyroid surgery but they would call and check and let me know. Later the medical facility called back and said the doctor would be glad to do it. The *person also had set up an appointment for me to see the doctor on June 5th at 4:00pm. The person asked me why am I going directly to surgery and I explained about the number of growths, the size of the larger one and my history. I hope this is the right choice; this doctor did a good job with my previous surgery but does he also have the experience in thyroid surgery? Some sources suggest that this surgery should have someone who does a lot of these, e.g. 50 or more a year. I have no way to judge this.*

Well, this has been a three-year ordeal with 4 ultrasounds and 1 biopsy on the thyroid ever since my heart doctor first discovered a growth on my thyroid. We are now on a different slope which culminates in surgery. This I suspect will also open a new experience as living without a thyroid or partial thyroid will require another drug to take as one cannot live without the hormones produced by the thyroid-thus the need for supplements. I am finding out that while surgery has its definite advantage to cure a problem it also results in some after-effects which are permanent.

This will be my 8th major surgery since my fall off the roof on August 12, 2000. No other major issues prior to that time.

Ever Forward (Roger)

As we continue to learn about the seemingly never-ending stream of bad news, we look at Bruce's life to learn how his character enabled him to continue moving forward. It would be an interesting debate as to which life experiences from Bruce's background formed his "ever forward" mentality: growing up on a dairy farm or the military?

Many years ago, a scientist by the name of Isaac Newton developed a theory that once a body is into motion, it stays in motion. Bruce most likely learned this theory in a science or physics class either in high school or while studying at Michigan State University.

Bruce turned this theory into one of his philosophies of life. For example: once he started working on a project, he continued until the project was finished. There were many opportunities for him to get distracted by a shiny new project, but Bruce ignored the new opportunities and continued forward on the current project. The only thing that stopped him while working on a project was the successful completion of that project.

While I was growing up Dad completed many projects around the house, the majority of which are still in existence because he moved forward in the right way; he didn't cut any corners. I still have a large, oak desk that he constructed 35+ years ago.

As you have read, there were many, many, many times when Bruce could have given up, but he resisted that urge. He moved forward.

When you get knocked down, it takes courage to get back up again. But it takes just as much courage to keep moving forward after you get back up.

The following was written by Bruce in the midst of the prostate fight, but is relevant to this period of his struggle as well. There is no doubt that his purpose in writing these words was to encourage others that they possessed the strength required to get up when they are knocked down and move on.

_____

"Moving On" (Bruce)

Freshly mowed, green, reaching to the blue.
There he comes, stands tall, ears pointed, alert,
Eyes sparkling, coat of brown, enjoying life.
Prancing, dancing, looking around, full of life.
Free to roam, off he goes,
Bringing joy.

Sheets of white, there he is, lying prone, wasting away.
Still alert, reminiscing, accepting, a twinkle in the eye,
Memories gone, coming back, seen a lot.
Hidden tears, wanting to break, life lived full.
Homeward bound, but not yet,
Giving joy.

Transparency separating, the free and the bound.
Outside and inside, neither right nor wrong,
One vertical, one horizontal,
One moving, one moving not,
Both are free,
Joy received.

Bruce W. VanderKolk (September 15, 2010)

June 7, 2012 (Bruce)

Saw the doctor today and surgery is set for July 16, 2012. The doctor agreed that waiting would be ok and also reaffirmed that if I have anaplastic cancer it isn't going to make any difference as that type is basically terminal and fast. If I have one of the other thyroid cancers then they have a very good cure rate and are slow growing. However, it was the doctor's opinion that based on the lack of symptoms, etc. that I do not have cancer. The doctor went through the risks which coincided with what I had read. These risks are:

1. Bleeding that can cause acute respiratory distress.
2. Injury to the recurrent laryngeal nerve that can cause permanent hoarseness.
3. Damage to the parathyroid glands that control calcium levels in the body, causing hypoparathyroidism and hypocalcemia.

The doctor said this is a serious and complicated surgery as there are so many aspects of the body that pass or exist in the neck region. From the nerves, arteries, throat, etc., it is all squeezed together and if there are growths such as what I have this compounds the problem. The doctor said the surgery is about 4 +/- hours. The doctor also explained how the surgery is done starting with about a 3-4 inch horizontal cut across the throat.

The doctor does worry about the operation as so many things can go wrong; one major aspect being removal or damage to the parathyroid glands. The other issues above are also a concern. In this operation the doctor said time is taken slowly.

The parathyroid gland is about the size of a grain of rice. There are four of these glands and they are located behind the thyroid gland. The purpose of these glands is to control the calcium levels in the body. These glands are important because calcium is extremely important to the body. The function of calcium is to:

1. Strengthen the skeletal system. We learned at a young age that calcium is necessary to build strong bones and that a lack of calcium could potentially lead to broken bones. Additionally, the body also uses bones to store calcium for other functions of the body.
2. Provide electrical energy for the nervous system. The nervous system uses calcium as a sort of conductor for electrical impulses to navigate throughout the nerves in the body. If the parathyroid glands are not

functioning properly, the nervous system is negatively affected resulting in a number of issues such as tiredness, weakness, etc.

3.   *Calcium also is necessary for the muscular system as it provides the energy necessary for the muscles to contract and work correctly. Weakness and potentially even cramping are symptoms of an improper amount of calcium in the muscular system.*

I will be having a total thyroidectomy, which removes all identifiable thyroid tissue.

I also obtained a copy of the recent ultrasound and ones from previous scans. My largest growth is solid and the other ones are a combination of cysts and solid nodes.

I would be less than truthful if I didn't mention that I am concerned about this surgery and the potential risks and negative outcomes. The doctor has performed about 20 of these which is not a lot. I hope the doctor is as good as we think he is.

Also read the official report from the ultrasound-copy given to me by a nurse after I asked for it. The results were:

1.   *Overall, the right thyroid lobe measures 5.2x1.8x1.8 cm. Within the upper pole is a 0.3 to 0.4 cm cystic nodule. Within the interpolar region is a 1.4x1.0x0.8 cm solid nodule. Within the lower pole are solid 1.4x1.0x0.9 cm and cystic 0.5x0.4x0.4 cm nodules.*

2.   *The thyroid isthmus is enlarged by a 4.4x3.8x2.0 cm heterogeneous echotexture solid nodule.*

3.   *The left thyroid lobe overall measures 5.1x2.3x1.9 cm. Within the interpolar region are solid 1.6x0.8x0.8 cm and 1.2x1.1x0.7 cm nodules. Within lower pole is a solid 1.0x0.7x0.7 cm nodule.*

June 11, 2012

Went to the doctor to get another shot in the right eye. The normal doctor was gone so I saw another doctor who had a better bedside manner. When this doctor gave me the shot I did not realize it was a shot and asked the doctor if I was going to get one. The doctor replied that it was done. The doctor also did not use the ring on the eye and I had very little discomfort on the way home. Afterwards I asked the receptionist at the registration desk if I could switch doctors. The receptionist went back to check and no one said "no" so my next appointment will be in 10 weeks with this new doctor. Did have something different as I was leaving and that was a large black spot on the bottom of my vision in the right eye. Went back up and asked them about it-appears it was a small air bubble and it went away in about 15 minutes.

Making Memories (Roger)

In the midst of all his health struggles, Dad and Mom still joined my brother and his family and myself for a family vacation in Colorado. We rented a house in Buena Vista with great scenic views of the mountains. We did the normal touristy activities: visited the local hot springs, experimented with fly fishing in the Arkansas River, went to Leadville for a touch of gambling, went hiking and mountain biking, made ourselves regulars at the local ice cream shop, rented ATV's and rode to the top of a mountain, and even went shooting at a public range that was the best range we ever experienced. We enjoyed spending time inside the house during meals, playing games, and laughing.

At no time during this vacation did Bruce complain or lament about his health problems.

He realized the trip wasn't about how he was feeling or his fears for the future. Dad realized that focusing on making memories was more important. Yet another example of how he Thrived during his struggle.

As you are going through your struggle, what memories are you making with your family? How about your friends?

July 18, 2012 (Bruce)

Well, the surgery is over and I am home. Actually came home in the afternoon of the 17th. Surgery was just over one hour as the doctor indicated the left and right side of the thyroid had shrunk and the center part with the growth came out easily. Have a very long cut across my neck. Sore, but not as bad as I thought I would be. Difficult to turn my neck and to look up. Did sleep in my bed last night and it wasn't too bad. Eating soft foods for now. Have started to take thyroid pills now. Jamie and his family came up to visit me after the surgery. They also brought me a stuffed cow. This will go along with the stuffed monkey I got from them after my prostate cancer surgery.

July 20, 2012

Saw the doctor today and the doctor thought everything looked good. My biopsy was negative. The doctor did say that one of the parathyroids was removed but the doctor is not concerned about that as I still have three left. The doctor also took out the internal stitches.

July 22, 2012

Helped Don (brother in law) some yesterday wrapping his deck. I was using the stapler and did something that really caused my neck to hurt in one area. Still bothers some today. Hopefully I did not tear something away now that the internal stitches are out. It also looks like there might be some more swelling but not sure. Roger stopped by last night and left after dinner today. Nice of him to do that. Saw the doctor a few days later as there was some swelling. The doctor said I had torn a small blood vessel.

Stubbornness (Roger)

One of Bruce's favorite stories from his youth had to do with a battle of wills between himself and his mother. There were likely numerous instances, but this particular episode focused on the dinner table one night. Bruce's mother had made hamburger for dinner and for whatever reason, young Bruce decided that he didn't want to eat said hamburger. The reason for his decision was that the ketchup used to make the hamburger was homemade rather than the store brand. Bruce was told that he couldn't get up from the table until he finished the meal. Needless to say he and his mother were at the dinner table for hours until she finally gave in and released him from the table to go to bed.

Stubbornness was engraved into Bruce's DNA. But where exactly does stubbornness come from? Where does the unshakable belief that our rightness is rooted in something greater than ourselves?

Bruce's writing during the previous eight months detailed many,

many challenges and just as many frustrations with the struggles that he was going through. The tone to the writings has definitely changed as well: there is a bent towards questioning why he was going through all of the struggles. You can almost hear him question aloud, "Wasn't the prostate cancer enough"?

This is common. If you are in the middle of a struggle, there is a good chance that you, too, have had, or are having, these feelings. Bruce's example showed us that there is hope on the other side of life's struggles. Not only did he write about the bad times, but he wrote about the good times also because he wanted everyone to realize that there WILL be good times throughout the journey. We simply have to keep pushing forward. While you might be in the trough of the wave cycle right now, the crest is coming.

As I have noted previously, music speaks to me. More specifically, the lyrics of music speak to me. I firmly believe Bruce would have embraced the latest album from David Crowder, "Milk and Honey" because it speaks to the glorious riches that await us when we put our faith in God. The Israelites went through many struggles when they left Egypt on their way to the Promised Land. Sure, many of them were self-inflicted, but they struggled nonetheless while they waited to cross over to the land of milk and honey.

The album would have resonated with the struggles that Bruce was undergoing and I hope it will resonate with your struggles as well.

When he was depressed and questioning why he was going through the struggles, the journals reflected his thoughts. But with his action, he pushed through the struggles with the same level of stubbornness that he displayed all those years ago at the kitchen table.

Bruce's stubbornness to keep going was rooted in his unwavering belief that God was bigger than his struggle. I wish he would have been able to read, reflect, and claim the words of another song in Crowder's album "Milk and Honey". The song "Who's Gonna Stop the King" speaks to the power provided by the King of the universe for those who have accepted Him and follow in His name.

There is a dichotomy with this power however, one that Bruce was familiar during his struggle, a dichotomy that is familiar with all those going through a serious medical struggle and are believers of

God and Jesus. The dichotomy for believers is whether to continue to struggle in this world or just give in and pass on to the glorious next one.

Bruce chose to fight, relying on the strength of The King, the one whose power cannot be matched by anyone on this world or in the next. The lyrics of the "Who's Gonna Stop the King" song are powerful. Listen to the song and take the lyrics to heart to help you during your struggle.

A Series of Events

Journal Gap (Roger)

There is a break in Bruce's journal for roughly 11 months, from July of 2012 to June of 2013. This is due to a diminishing of the wave cycles: There are still ups and downs of course as Bruce learned to live with an altered body but during that time, major issues or complications were kept at bay. It was a "Pax Bruce" if you will: Bruce and his body were relatively at peace with each other. Ever the military historian, Bruce probably would have classified the period as more akin to the Korean conflict: Both parties were still at odds as they eyed each other across the DMZ.

But as the calendar neared the second half of 2013, Bruce's body was tired of all the waiting and decided to prepare to cross the line of demarcation. His body was getting ready for war.

June 26, 2013 (Bruce)

Saw the skin doctor today about a spot that had been growing on my left arm near the wrist. The doctor thought it was a squamous cell carcinoma and removed it for a biopsy. Report came back the following week confirming that it was cancer and it was a squamous cell carcinoma. This is a step up in skin cancer for me as all the other ones had been basal cell. Squamous cell can spread to other parts of the body if not caught early. The doctor said this one was small and no need for additional treatment.

Sept 15, 2013

Went biking in the afternoon and on the road out of town I took a good crash as I was going across the railroad track. The track runs at an angle and I hit it wrong. Landed on my head and other parts. Face and hand were bleeding and I knew I was in trouble. Finally dragged my bike off the road and after calming down called Donna to come and get me. We went to the local medical facility.

The official report was concussion, bruises and contusions to right shoulder, right hand, left hand and fingers, left knee, right side of face. Had a CT and X-rays but they did not show any breaks. Right hand is useless and left knee is not good.

Journaling (Roger)

There is an old adage: Things are always darkest before the storm. But how exactly does one define "darkest"? Specifically for Bruce, were things darkest when he was fighting prostate cancer? Or were they darkest when he was fighting prostate cancer and an unknown thyroid issue? Or when he had (seemingly) overcome both of those issues and now was faced with another occurrence of skin cancer and a fairly major bicycle accident?

Or would they become darkest in a few days time when he would receive other bad and potentially life-altering news?

The answer of course is that "darkest" varies for all of us. My darkest will be different from Bruce's. Your darkest will be different from mine or from Bruce's. During this life, we will all experience unique circumstances, experiences, and challenges. This is both a blessing and a curse: sometimes life makes us feel like we are alone in our darkest struggles with no escape.

During these times, we need a plan on how to approach and deal with life during the darkest struggles.

One of the things that helped Bruce navigate these darkest times is by writing the journal that you are reading. This journaling process was therapeutic to Bruce in a variety of ways:

1. Journaling allowed him to sort through his feelings. I cannot imagine all of the feelings that Dad went through during his various struggles. The constant, never-ending waves of emotions could have been debilitating and a reason to curse God and withdraw from society. Instead, by putting his feelings into words on the computer screen, he was able to realize that while his feelings were normal, he must not dwell on the negative feelings. Journaling helped him to focus on the positive and be a blessing to his family, to his friends, to his church, and even to people he didn't know.

2. It allowed him to focus on what is important. Speaking of being a blessing to others, that's really what we are here for on earth, is it not? In our society we all get caught up in our careers, climbing the corporate ladder, and making enough money to ensure that we will be able to have a long and comfortable retirement. But if you really think about it, our purpose here is to help improve the lives of others. The purpose of parents is to improve the lives of their children. The purpose of having friends is to improve the lives of each other during daily life and through struggles. There are countless ways to volunteer to help the lives of the less fortunate which also helps us live out our purpose. Throughout his battles and struggle with cancers and various other illnesses, Bruce routinely volunteered at the local homeless shelter to improve, if even for just a little, the lives of those less fortunate. If the focus of your journal is 100% about you, then it may be time for a readjustment in what is really important in this life.

3. Journaling allowed him to document his experience to help others in the future. As a family, we have discussed this repeatedly: Why did Bruce keep a journal of his experiences? We firmly believe that Bruce's intent was to reach outside of himself and use his experience as an example to others that are also going through similar struggles. As humans, when something bad happens to us, we tend to believe that we are the ONLY ones that have ever experienced that situation. The truth is, that is a lie, and we have to stop telling ourselves this lie. Bruce realized this inconvenient lie and wanted to share how he navigated his struggle with his head held high. He wanted to be an example to others so that they could also thrive through their struggle.

Speaking of journals and struggles: Are you going through a struggle? I encourage you to begin a journal to record the happenings in your life, your feelings, your emotions, your responses, and the path forward. Often you capture your thoughts when you reflect on the journal. Your journal will likely be very different from Bruce's and that is perfectly ok. It will be very personal, and likely not something ready for prime time and to be published. But the benefits are significant because the journal will help you focus on thriving during your difficult time. Journaling can help keep track of time lines and details that might be hard to hold onto when faced with stress or grief.

Sept 17, 2013 (Bruce)

Swelling badly on right hand and going up arm. Went to see a doctor at the local medical facility. The doctor took more X-rays but still did not show any breaks. Just bad soft tissue and ligament damage. Asked that I see another doctor on Sept 19, 2013. At home I looked at my helmet and saw where it had been damaged and there was a deep gouge in it about ½ inch wide and ¼ inch deep. Without the helmet that would have been my head.

Sept 19, 2013

Saw a new doctor. Gave me a brace for right hand which really helps ease the pain. Also said it would be several weeks in healing and that these injuries take longer than a break. Also mentioned that my CT showed a nodule in my thyroid area which is odd because I had that all removed last July 2012. The doctor said it could be scar tissue but wanted me to get an ultrasound in the future. I mentioned that I was seeing another doctor on Sept 26, 2013, and the doctor said I should disclose the information at that time. If the other doctor wanted to do the ultrasound that was OK. This doctor also said I was lucky that I did not sustain more serious injuries-the doctor also said to get a new helmet.

Hobbies (Roger)

Bruce's love affair with the bicycle began in Wheaton, IL around 1973/1974. Donna volunteered with the Pioneer Girls and one day the troop took a bike hike. Bruce and Donna were hooked; they jumped at the chance to purchase used bikes when friends were looking to upgrade and were going to sell their old bikes. Together Bruce and Donna spent countless hours touring both near and far on bicycles. This passion was also passed to their sons, both of whom continue biking thousands of miles a year to this day.

Bruce always felt alive on the bicycle. Being able to be outside, experiencing God's creation while feeling the rushing of the air was something that he enjoyed. It is unknown the total miles he biked throughout his life, but at minimum, it must have been enough to circle the globe (24,901 miles).

There are risks in cycling, especially where Bruce lived. Rarely was he able to take the bicycle out on dedicated bike paths where there was no fear or risk of being hit by an automobile. While living in central Illinois, Bruce lived outside the city limits and spent most of his bicycling time on country roads. If you've not experienced country road traffic, the cars are usually traveling at high rates of speed with few concerns for pedestrian and bicycle traffic. The same was true when he moved to northern Illinois: No bike paths, so he was forced to travel on country roads or county highways.

Bruce therefore had a saying about bicycling: "It's not IF you get into an accident; it is a matter of WHEN you'll get into an accident". And true to his word, he was involved in quite a few accidents while out on his bicycle.

Despite this, Bruce persisted and continued bicycling. The rewards outweighed the risk. Being outside, feeling the air rush past him, while he communed with God and Creation, were worth the risk of getting into an accident.

Even when he crashed while crossing a railroad track, he would count down the days until he could get back on the bicycle again. It was something he looked forward to while in the midst of his struggles, something that he would be able to get back and enjoy. All he had to do was to make it through his struggles.

Later in life Dad was drawn towards hobbies that engaged his artistic nature. He began writing; not only journaling, but also some poetry as well. A few of these poems are included in this book. He invested in a good camera and used it to capture natural beauty in wildlife and animals.

The following written work is a combination of two of those hobbies: photography and poetry. Dad created a photo book with poetry to capture the magnificence of God's Creation.

The introduction of the book is as follows:

"Are you really in tuned with God's creation,
Or do you see it without seeing.
Do you marvel at the intricacies revealed,
Of a spider's interwoven web.

Are you in awe of the color
Of leaves in the Fall.
Or the gracefulness of a snowflake
As it slowly makes it fall.

Have you ever stopped to study ants
As they work by some inner design.
Or a flock of geese as they travel overhead,
Flying in unison by an internal GPS.

Maybe you've seen the helix
That describes who we are.
Or walked the fields of grain,
And marveled at the waves.

Have you searched the grass
For the perfect clover four.
Or watched the monarch
With it's colorful grace.

Whatever your case may be,
Open your eyes and let them see.
As we take a journey,
And see what you have not seen.

And as we travel, whatever you see,
Ask yourself, can this really be by chance.
Are the majestic colors and symmetry just random design
Or is there a higher power that eliminates chance."
(Bruce VanderKolk)

We all have hobbies. Some are constructive while some are just diversions from our reality. The constructive hobbies are gifts; they help us to focus on something other than the struggles we are going through. They give us something to look forward to participating in again.

Following in Bruce's footsteps, it probably comes as no surprise that my hobby is bicycling. When trouble comes calling, my biking miles significantly increase as I spend more time on the bike, refocusing my mind, communing with nature, and spending time in meditation and prayer with God.

It may seem frivolous to some to think about hobbies when in the midst of a trial or struggle, but they can actually be a blessing. Allowing your mind a brief respite from your challenges is healthy. It can even help you gain perspective. Maintaining a hobby can also help you keep a sense of identity. It can remind you of who you were before or aside from the challenge you face.

What is your hobby? Specifically, what is your constructive hobby that will help refocus your mind during your struggle?

October 8, 2013 (Bruce)

Saw the doctor today and my fasting sugar count was 110 but my A1C was 6.4. As a result the doctor has considered me to be pre-diabetic and has placed me on a drug to try and lower my sugar readings. One more pill and something else to contend with.

October 14, 2013

Ultrasound of thyroid at a local medical facility.

October 17, 2013

Had an ultrasound done on my throat Monday (14 October 2013) at a local medical facility. This was requested by the new doctor after I mentioned about the CT scan and what the previous doctor said on Sept 19, 2013. Today the new doctor called me and said there were several nodules some larger than 1cm. The doctor did not understand why they were there if I had a total thyroidectomy last year. *The doctor gave some options such as having a biopsy or surgery. I choose the biopsy, however, Donna thought I should have surgery. I called back to the doctor and asked him what would be his choice of options. The doctor said surgery. I am now scheduled to see the doctor tomorrow at 10:00a to discuss where to have the surgery. I am not going back to the previous medical facility for this surgery. I need to find out more about other nearby medical facilities.*

I obtained a copy of the doctor's surgery report from my operation last year in July. It states that I had a total thyroidectomy

Again I must ask myself does it ever quit? Can I go for at least a year without having more medical issues? Why do some people seem to be free from medical issues but others are not? I am really frustrated at this point and not pleased at all with what the previous doctor did. Maybe there is an answer to how the nodules came back but will ask that question tomorrow when I meet with the current doctor.

If it had not been for the bike accident I would not be aware of the thyroid problem. Was the accident a blessing in disguise and the hand of God was in it? I find it very hard to believe in coincidences.

October 18, 2013

Donna and I met with the current doctor at the medical facility at 10:30am. We discussed the findings of the ultrasound in which it showed a thyroid present. This was to have been removed by the previous doctor in 2012 and in which that doctor stated to us that it had been removed. This doctor was at a loss as to how this could have happened. We discussed options and the doctor mentioned having a biopsy or having a second operation. The doctor believes that because of the radiation exposure I had, plus the presence of nodules, and the fact that the thyroid is still present, I should have the surgery. I said ok and was referred to yet another doctor to do the surgery.

October 21, 2013

Called an attorney about a potential medical malpractice suit. Explained the situation about the original doctor not taking out the thyroid but stated in the surgery report that the doctor had done a total thyroidectomy. The attorney recommended a different attorney. Spoke with this second attorney and was told that I should gather up all reports from the doctors and the medical facilities. This was done and delivered to the attorney's office on the Oct 22, 2013.

Summary of meeting with yet another doctor at yet another medical facility.

This doctor stated there is still a Thyroid present. I gave the doctor a copy of original doctor's surgical report and this doctor read it while we waited. This doctor stated that it was difficult to explain why the surgical doctor missed taking out the thyroid. This doctor can speculate but cannot explain the situation. This doctor found a couple aspects of the surgical doctor's report interesting such as how the surgical doctor saw the nerves because the nerves are usually deep and behind the thyroid but yet failed to remove the left and right lobes. This doctor also could not ascertain exactly what the surgical doctor removed based on the report nor could this doctor tell from the pathology report.

The doctor stated because there has already been one surgery on the thyroid an additional surgery would be of high risk. Therefore there does not appear to be a good solution to this issue but there are options. The doctor also asked me if the previous doctor did any follow up after the surgery such as an additional ultrasound and the answer is no. The options are:

1. *Do nothing-this is really not a viable option as there is still a thyroid present with nodules that were not taken care of in 2012 by the previous doctor. Additionally this doctor, based upon my history of exposure to radiation to the neck and head area plus the fact that the recommendation for removal in 2012 was not followed, recommends that a total thyroidectomy be accomplished now.*

2. *Extensive radiation with radioactive potassium iodine to kill the thyroid. The doctor said this is not a very good option and would not recommend it.*

3. *Surgery to remove the thyroid. As stated earlier this is a high risk surgery because of scar tissue and potential complications with scar tissue interfering in the surgery, more possibility of damaging the vocal cord, and removing or killing the parathyroid (one parathyroid was already accidentally removed by the previous doctor; that leaves three more and there is no way of determining at this time where they are or if they have already been damaged). This doctor stated that the body needs at least a half of a parathyroid to function properly. The parathyroid controls the calcium level in the body and without parathyroids there is a large problem. The doctor would be willing to perform this surgery but wanted us to know the risks. The doctor would also send me to an ENT specialist to do a scope to determine if there has already been any damage to the vocal cords prior to any surgery. The doctor asked me if I thought my voice had changed after*

the previous surgery and I mentioned I thought there was some change and mentioned it to the previous doctor. That doctor believed I sounded the same. This is documented in one of the previous doctor's reports.

4. *Performing a biopsy of the two largest nodules. The typical method is by FNA (Fine Needle Aspiration) which gathers thyroid cells. However, this doctor uses a slightly larger needle and obtains a core sample. This helps to have a larger sample to send to pathology and less of a possibility of not getting the cancer if it is present. This doctor also would attempt to do the two nodules but because of the prior surgery there is a possibility that the doctor could not do a biopsy on both nodules. I asked the doctor if there is still a possibility of missing a cancer and the answer was yes but it is diminished with the core sample procedure. It was this doctor's recommendation that we first do this option because of the risk of doing surgery. If the sample is cancerous there is no choice but to follow up with surgery. If the sample is inconclusive we would need to rethink about surgery. If the sample is negative, there would be a need for continuous monitoring with additional screening and possibly a yearly biopsy.*

Based upon the above scenarios, of which none are very encouraging, and selecting the option with the least possible risk at this time, I concurred with doing the biopsy. We also discussed the fact that this goes contrary to another doctor's recommendation. However, this doctor would be the one that must do the surgery and if it can be avoided because of the high risk potential, the biopsy should be considered as the first course of action.

We also discussed other issues such as this doctor's background and experience, the CT scan done after my bike accident which found a suspicious area in the thyroid area and the other doctor's recommendation for follow-up, how the surgery is performed and the biopsy, speculation as to how the previous doctor could have missed taking out the total thyroid, the situation in which I was exposed to radiation and how it leads to cancer in the thyroid, etc.

From my perspective, there is not a good solution to the problem created by the previous doctor. It certainly has raised my anxiety and frustration as well as my wife's anxiety. It is difficult not to have this on my mind and worry about the consequences. Having been through a thyroid biopsy I have found it is not a pleasant procedure. I certainly do not want to have a second thyroid surgery not only because of the risks to the throat area but also because of the risks in having any surgery.

Perseverance (Roger)

Are you familiar with the book of Job from the Bible? The book of Job is really just a story of a person known as, you guessed it, Job. The book begins by describing the success that Job had developed throughout his life: Big family, rich, the "greatest man among all the people of the East" (Job 1:1, NIV).

The book then describes a discussion between the devil and God that the only reason people feared (ie: loved) God was that they wanted to be wealthy. The devil said that if everything was taken away from Job, he would curse God. God said you're wrong but you can do what you want to test Job. So the devil did exactly that.

The next 40 chapters are the lamentations of Job during which he never curses God.

Job perseveres.

At some level, Bruce had to draw a comparison between himself and Job. He surely must have asked "Why am I being tested?" and "When will it end?". Just consider the frustration with going through a major surgery, the only reason of it was to remove an organ. That was the only reason. Then to be told several months later that whoops, the organ is still there. That alone is enough to drive all but the strongest person to their knees, begging for clarity, for some sense of purpose, for a rationale of going through the first surgery.

If we are being honest with ourselves, most of us would have been angry. And justifiably so. Angry at the doctor. Angry at the medical facility. Angry at the disease. Angry at our body.

And more than likely, angry with God. Would we fall to the temptation of cursing God for putting us through the situation? Or would we be like Job?

Bruce emulated Job. He simply moved on. He persevered. Was he angry? Absolutely. Did he lash out at God. Probably. But did he let his situation disrupt his mission of being an example so that others could see God?

No. Bruce persevered.

October 27, 2013 (Bruce)

Today marks 6 weeks since I had my bike accident. Most areas are healed up but left knee is still stiff and sore when I put pressure on it such as kneeling down. The worst is still my right hand as I still cannot close it and it is very stiff and can feel it in fingers and the hand. Not sure there has been much improvement over the last few weeks. Still going to Physical Therapy and doing the exercises. I am beginning to wonder if it will ever be the same.

October 29, 2013

Saw a doctor today about my the spot on my lip. The doctor did a biopsy and I go back Nov 5 to find out the results and have the three stitches removed.

October 30, 2013

The new doctor did my thyroid biopsy today. The doctor also showed me on the ultrasound today (which is part of the procedure) that not only were the left and right lobes present but also the isthmus. This doctor has not seen anything like this and doesn't know what the previous doctor might have removed although there was a pathology report from last year. We discussed if it could have grown back and the answer is no. This doctor took three samples from the left lobe and five samples from the right lobe.

November 4, 2013

Saw a doctor today about my shoulder and right hand. This was a follow up after doing physical therapy. The shoulder is better. The hand still has some swelling and I cannot yet make a complete fist. It has been 7 weeks and 1 day. Looks like the hand may take several more weeks. I am to continue the exercises learned at physical therapy.

Received a call from the new doctor and my thyroid biopsy samples were all negative. We discussed what next and decided to wait and watch. I am to call the doctor in six months and schedule another ultrasound. This doctor would remove it to give me peace of mind but I have always been told to avoid surgery if you possibly can. God answered this prayer in that it was not cancer.

November 6, 2013

I thought it was appropriate to hold off on writing for the remainder of 2013. Hopefully there will not be anything new to add for a few years and this journal will not continue.

December 1, 2013

I guess waiting until 2014 is not going to be an option. On November 16, 2013, I started a treatment on my lower lip for cancer and pre-cancer cells. The treatment is a chemotherapy that I apply twice a day. The first week wasn't bad and I began to wonder if it was working. However, this past week has been different as my lip is starting to show the effects and is cracking and blistering. It is really sore and hard to bite into any food. I apply a petroleum jelly to the lips which helps but only for a few hours. I am also taking an over-the-counter medicine for the pain. I looked up the drug on the Internet and saw pictures of other people. What I am going through is normal and my lips look just like the pictures. I quit the process last night but probably should continue it until Friday which will be three weeks-that is how long I was to do the treatments. Maybe I am just a big baby but it is miserable.

December 4, 2013

Well, I continued the process and have only two more days left. Miserable. Hard to sleep and I get up every two hours to put more petroleum jelly on the lips. Made an appointment to see a doctor on December 5, 2013 just to make sure everything is ok and to get established down in Florida with a doctor. Seem to need to see this type of doctor about every 3-4 months now.

December 5, 2013

Saw a new doctor today in the town where we will be in Florida. The doctor thought the lip looked ok but after seeing where I had also applied the chemo to the left side of my face the doctor wanted me to do 3 weeks on all of my face and ears. Also showed the doctor a mole on my left arm which I think was changing in appearance plus a spot on my right hand. The doctor removed both for a biopsy.

December 9, 2013

Found out my PSA test which I had done last week came back as undetectable. This makes four years of prostate cancer free. Great news. Thank you, God.

December 10, 2013

Received a call from the doctor about my biopsy. The area on my right hand was negative. The mole on my left arm was positive for pre-cancer. They want me to come back in on January 23, 2014 to have that taken care of; probably by liquid nitrogen freezing. Did not ask what type of cancer that might have turned into-will do when I see the doctor. This is first time I have had a pre-cancer mole.

Get up and Fight (Roger)

The hits keep coming, but Bruce keeps getting back up after getting hit. He is struggling with all the negative news and developments, but is still in the fight.

We've all seen movies where characters are knocked down. In boxing or fighting movies, the characters who have been knocked down are told to "stay down". Do they listen? Nope. They struggle and get back on their feet. And sometimes they get knocked back down again. But eventually, they get up and, surprise, surprise, win the fight. In one of my favorite movies depicting soldiers, one of the main characters is pretty roughed up and asked if he was "still in the fight". His response? Still in the fight.

Who knows where Bruce got that type of spirit. Perhaps it was a result of growing up on the dairy farm where he would get knocked around by the animals but yet still have to finish his chores. Perhaps it was the "ever-forward" mentality that was drilled into him during his time in the military.

Let's go back to the boxing analogy. What happens when the knocked fighter gets back up? Does he jump right back up, ready for the fight? Not often. Usually what happens is that the person struggles to get up and relies on the ropes to pull himself up and steady himself for the fight.

The How is not important. What is important is that Bruce took the hits from the various diseases and kept getting back up to stay in the fight that we know as life.

How about you? Are you getting up after being knocked down? It's tough for sure. It will seem impossible. But it's necessary in order to walk through the valley and come out the other side.

Who are your ropes? Family? Friends? Lean on them. Let them help you as you struggle to get back into the fight.

The Bible speaks to this type of spirit in 2 Corinthians 11:22-27:

"Are they Hebrews? So am I. Are they Israelites? So am I. Are they Abraham's descendants? So am I. Are they servants of Christ? (I am out of my mind to talk like this.) I am more. I have worked much harder, been in prison more frequently, been flogged more severely, and been exposed to death again and again. Five times I received from the Jews the forty lashes minus one. Three times I was beaten with rods, once I was pelted with stones, three times I was shipwrecked, I spent a night and a day in the open sea, I have been constantly on the move. I have been in danger from rivers, in danger from bandits, in danger from my fellow Jews, in danger from Gentiles; in danger in the city, in danger in the country, in danger at sea; and in danger from false believers. I have labored and toiled and have often gone without sleep; I have known hunger and thirst and have often gone without food; I have been cold and naked." (NIV)

Despite all of the turmoil and strife that the apostle Paul suffered throughout his ministry, he endured and was a driving force in Christianity. How many people would not know the Lord today if he had simply quit the ministry after the first shipwreck?

Do you have a relationship with God? He is the best supporter of all to help you get through your struggles and get back into the fight.

December 13, 2013 (Bruce)

Well this is day 8 of doing the chemo on my whole face. It has been one week since I started and it is really starting to show the bad cells, particularly around my nose. I expected the forehead to be the worst but does not look like that will be the case. Starting to hurt, particularly to the touch and when I try to sleep with the CPAC breathing machine. Looks like it is going to be many more poor nights of sleeping. The lip is starting to look a little better but it is still sore. Going to the pharmacy today to see if there is anything I can put on the face so that it does not hurt as much.

Well the pharmacist said I should talk to the Dr. So I called and the nurse said do not put anything on except petroleum jelly. Other things cause reaction and interference. After the treatment is over I might be able to get something to ease the soreness.

December 17, 2013

Well, it is day 12 of the treatments. I no longer can use my CPAC breathing machine as the mask is unbearable. People are really starting to notice and ask questions. A friend at church Monday said people who look like me in Florida either have a bad sunburn or are doing the chemo treatment. She was very perceptive.

The worst is the nose and on both sides of the nose. Very tender to the touch. The lip is starting to heal up and I only have a portion of the scab that I had before. Maybe another week and the lip will be ok.

Relationships (Roger)

There is now about a five month gap in Bruce's journal. Did everything heal up and all of the pain go away? Absolutely not because he was still going through the chemo treatments on his face while in Florida. The same treatments that were aggravated by the sun. It's safe to say that he was miserable as the Florida sun seemed relentless throughout the month of December and into the new year.

No, the more appropriate answer is that Bruce decided to put his struggles on the back burner and focus on spending quality time with family and friends over the Christmas and New Year's holidays.

Mom and Dad were in Florida that winter so I went down to visit them over the holidays. We made the most of the time together: We took a swamp boat tour of the Everglades, toured the Vizcaya house near Miami, and even went for a jet boat ride off of Miami Beach. We also spent a lot of time with friends including spending New Year's Eve with the minister and his family. Then after the holidays Dad and Mom were in a warm climate spending time with old friends and making new friends.

The takeaway from those couple of weeks was that Dad focused on how to be a blessing to others rather than worrying about his own health.

Did he struggle? Absolutely. Just ask Donna. (Just kidding. Don't ask her). But more times than not, Bruce was focusing on making good memories with his family and having good visits. More times than not, Bruce focused on enriching the lives of friends and acquaintances during visits and times of fellowship.

Bruce's action of placing his worries, pains, and struggles behind him and celebrating the lives of others exemplified what it means to thrive:

Focus Externally.

Not Internally.

April 28, 2014 (Bruce)

Received a call today from a medical facility that the spot removed last week, April 23, 2014, was basal cell skin cancer. This is my fifth skin cancer, four basal cell and one squamous cell. The doctor wants to have me come in on May 13th, 2014 to make sure the doctor got it all. I never saw this spot as it was on my upper left shoulder. Go in Friday to have the stitches out.

On April 30th I go to have a larger growth removed from my upper right arm on the inside. It is about the size of a quarter, at least looking at it. The doctor does not think it is cancer but may be a Lipoma, which is a fatty growth.

April 30, 2014

Had the growth on the inside of my right arm removed today by the doctor. It was about the size of a grape with about a ¾ inch finger from it. The doctor showed it to me and it was interesting. Had its own covering. I expected it to be part of the other tissue but it wasn't. Will not know result of biopsy until next week.

May 9, 2014

Saw a new doctor today. Nice person and was originally from an area near where I lived in Michigan. The doctor also knew the two doctors that were working my prostate issues. Good news as my PSA was undetectable. It has been 4 ½ years now since my surgery for prostate cancer.

Also received a letter from the doctor that removed the growth from my arm: my growth was a Lipoma and was not cancer. Another good news.

May 13, 2014

Today I went in to have more of the basal cell cancer removed from my left shoulder. *The doctor mentioned that I had a pigmented basal cell which explains why the biopsy mentioned that melanin was found. At home I researched the pigmentation and found that the color it exhibits can be the same as for a melanoma skin cancer. The doctor explained that because of the appearance and color of the spot the doctor had to approach the biopsy as if it was a melanoma. Evident that is why the doctor took a deep plug rather than a scraping.*

Well it took an hour to remove the remaining cancer. Of this time about ¾ of an hour was the actual operation. The doctor removed about 1 ½ inches of tissue in a circular manner. I am not sure how deep, however, the doctor had to do internal stitches and about 8 external stitches. They put a big pressure bandage on it so to help stop the bleeding after the doctor had done the stitches. Again, was I surprised. I expected maybe a ½ inch as this has been the pattern with my skin cancers. I never expected such a large amount to be taken. The doctor sent it to the pathology lab to make sure all of it was removed and it was all basal cell. Should find out next week about the results.

On my previous visit the doctor took a picture of the spot during the biopsy. I asked to look at it so maybe next time I could recognize that a spot looks suspicious. Looking at the spot it was hard to believe that what was hard to see, at least for me, turned into a major removal of tissue.

I am finding that my rate of skin cancer is increasing as well as pre-cancer spots which have been removed. It is difficult to go six months without the need to remove some tissue. Is this another agent orange situation? I have read just recently about a new study that did link agent orange to skin cancer, however, at this time it is not classified as such by the VA.

Clinging to Hope (Roger)

At this point in life, during the 4+ years from 2009-2014, Bruce had his share of physical battles. He had fought, or was still fighting:

- Prostate cancer
- Growths on thyroid
- Heart concern
- Skin cancer
- Effects from prostate removal
- Hernia surgery

- Second hernia surgery
- Eye stroke treatment - shots into the eyeball
- Eye stroke effects - basic blindness in right eye
- Growths on and around thyroid
- Thyroid removal
- Skin cancer
- Bike crash: concussion, bruises, multiple contusions
- Pre-diabetes
- Thryoid is back
- Cancer on lip
- Skin cancer on face
- Skin cancer on torso

Personally, if I had to go through only one of these issues I would probably curl up in a ball and cry.

But despite all of the brutal waves life was putting him through, Bruce still made the choice to cling to his faith, his anchor. You see, his faith told him that all of the troubles, all of the constant and never ending periods of ups and down waves, his hope was secure in God. Every day he clung to that hope.

Bruce's hope in God was rooted in scripture:

Hebrews 10:23 (NIV)

"Let us hold unswervingly to the hope we profess, for he who promised is faithful."

Psalm 63 (NIV)

"A psalm of David. When he was in the Desert of Judah.
You, God, are my God,
   earnestly I seek you;
I thirst for you,
   my whole being longs for you,
in a dry and parched land
   where there is no water.
I have seen you in the sanctuary
   and beheld your power and your glory.

Because your love is better than life,
   my lips will glorify you.
I will praise you as long as I live,
   and in your name I will lift up my hands.
I will be fully satisfied as with the richest of foods;
   with singing lips my mouth will praise you.
On my bed I remember you;
   I think of you through the watches of the night.
Because you are my help,
   I sing in the shadow of your wings.
I cling to you;
   your right hand upholds me.
Those who want to kill me will be destroyed;
   they will go down to the depths of the earth.
They will be given over to the sword
   and become food for jackals.
But the king will rejoice in God;
   all who swear by God will glory in him,
   while the mouths of liars will be silenced."

As we wrap up this part of Bruce's story, there is another song by Crowder in the "Milk and Honey" album that speaks to the hope that Bruce lived. The title of the song is "Better Than Sunshine". The words of the song beautifully describe the hope that Bruce clung to all day, every day. Because of the everlasting, eternal ramifications of the choice that he made all those years ago, Bruce's life, no matter how dark the cancer made it seem, was going to lead to everlasting glory.

That day when Dad chose to accept Jesus Christ as his Lord and Savior was truly better than the best day we could ever possibly have on this earth.

———————————————————

Conclusion

Legacy

I know most of you did not know Bruce and couldn't differentiate between him and Adam. To our family, he was father, husband, brother, and friend. To his friends, he was someone who could be trusted to bend over backwards to help a buddy out, starting in the military all the way to the end of his time here on earth.

I didn't see Dad at work, except for the rare times that we would stop by to take him out to lunch. I definitely didn't see him at work in his capacity with the military and the National Guard. There was some overlap with his responsibilities at church, but many of those meetings were held in the evening while I was working or at home doing homework.

But I didn't have to see him with his work or volunteer hat on to realize that the vast majority of the people working for him in all of his capacities had positive experiences with Bruce. He was thrown retirement parties at all the career paths he endeavored from the National Guard, the Illinois State Police, to the Church. Bruce was honored by all when he left.

When he passed away, we held two memorial services, one in Florida and one in central Illinois. There were a number of people in the Illinois service who were positively touched by Bruce at some point during their lives. The amount of positive comments to the family was tremendous. He truly was a leader of people.

Likewise, many people in the Florida service also expressed their positive interactions with Bruce. It is important to remember that these interactions took place while Bruce was battling the illnesses as outlined in this book.

Despite the illnesses. Despite feeling beaten down and abused. Despite everything, Bruce made it his mission to make positive contributions on those around him.

Bruce thrived.

Epilogue

Bruce's journey is not finished. After successfully dealing with skin cancer, the thyroid issues, and finally prostate cancer, Bruce enjoyed a period of time marked by just a few smaller medical issues.

That period was shattered however in 2014 when Bruce was informed that there were issues with his bladder. That journey is both similar and unique from the prostate journey. Dad fought bladder cancer for 3+ years and recorded his experience, thoughts, and emotions into his journal. It will be a focus of the next book in the series, "Thriving Amidst Bladder Cancer: A General's Continued Fight". Look for it online or navigate to our website for more information: www.blauwshackmedia.com.

PART FOUR

AFTERWORD

Personal Note

This has been a difficult book to write. The process of going through dad's writings has opened fresh wounds caused by losing a beloved family member unexpectedly and too soon.

Dad's passing left his family and close friends in a state of complete shock. We all felt that if there was anyone who could outlast cancer, it was Dad. Everyone believed that Bruce's mission on earth wasn't finished; he had a lot more of himself to give the church, his friends, acquaintances, and yes, his family. More than once, the question, "What would Bruce have done?" was asked at home or at a leadership level at the church. His loss left a huge void in the lives of many. Including mine.

However, after navigating through life without him here for three years, it is time. It is time to make his dream a reality. After spending many hours pouring through his journals, it is absolutely certain that Dad's intent with the journals was to be a blessing to others. We can only hope that this book will help accomplish his dream.

Thank you for taking this journey with me.

I hope this book has been a blessing to you and that you join Bruce on the journey through bladder cancer in an upcoming book.

Acknowledgments

First and foremost, I have to express my forever gratitude to my father, Bruce VanderKolk. Even after he has passed, he continues to help me on my journey through this experience we call life. I was blessed beyond measure to be raised in a home where both parents were believers. They did everything in their power to ensure that their children were given everything necessary to push them on their faith journey to become children of God.

The bulk of this book is taken from the journal Dad wrote during all of his battles with cancer and other serious illnesses. How he was able to sit at his computer and type these words are beyond my comprehension. He fought through physical ailments and mental anguish at reliving the situations as he wrote his journal.

The book itself is a result of Mom's simple question: "Why not take Dad's journal and turn it into a book? Surely it could help people." This was late 2021, three and a half years after Bruce had passed. His passing was such a shock that we are just now coming to grips with it and are able to spend blocks of time thinking about him without breaking down. None of us had actually been able to read his journal until this year. Thanks, Mom, for everything: You gave us life, nurtured us, pointed us in the right direction to go in life, and made sure that we developed a relationship with God so that one day, we will see Dad again. You were absolutely correct: Dad would have wanted this journal to be made available to others.

I also would like to thank Jeff and Judy Chitwood, ministers to our family for over 30+ years. We owe such a debt of gratitude towards the guidance, ministry, love, support, encouragement, leadership, and friendship that both of you have shown to my family. We are blessed that God led us to the church in Springfield so many years ago. Jeff, your review of the verses included in the Guide to Thriving section and suggestion of more appropriate verses is greatly appreciated.

Thanks to those of you who reviewed early copies of the manuscript: Donna, James, Shelia, Mary Lou, Don, Sandy, Greg, Kathryn, Dennis, Judy, Steve, Tammy, Jeff, and Dawn. Your suggestions made this a better book.

And finally, and certainly not least, I need to thank Donna Hutcherson for lending your editing experience to this book. Your insight and suggestions took this from a collection of thoughts about Dad's journal into a piece that is publishable. Thank you for all the suggestions, the discussion, and yes, even all the corrections that I had to make after your reviews.

PART FIVE

GUIDE TO THRIVING

Introduction

By and large, Bruce approached life from a military point of view: It is better to be prepared and not require the plan than to need the plan and not be prepared. This mentality served him well as he fought through all of the serious illnesses as outlined in this book.

The purpose of his journal is to equip those going through similar struggles by pulling lessons from Bruce's life. This section of the book is meant to provide an opportunity to focus on those lessons and consider their application to the life of the reader.

I encourage you to consider this book as a regular resource as you walk through your valley and fight to Thrive in the midst of your struggle. This section is a summary of the lessons on thriving pulled from Bruce's life; there are 21 such lessons. I encourage you to read and meditate / pray on each lesson. At the conclusion of each lesson a blank space is provided for you to write encouragements to your future self so that you can continue to thrive amidst your journey.

———————————————

1. Seek The Light

<u>Key to Thriving:</u>

Recognize your need for faith; we are made to worship the Creator of the heavens and the earth. Specifically, faith in Jesus Christ as outlined in the Bible. This key to thriving is so vitally important that it goes beyond simply reading the Bible however. Find a church to learn and grow in your faith with a community of like-minded people. Pray that God would make Himself known to you.

If you have faith, make it stronger. Read your Bible. Find a devotional book that speaks to your heart and journey. Fellowship with other believers.

If your faith if faltering because of your struggles, realize that this is normal as evidenced in Bruce's journal. It is ok to question your lot in life. Follow the ideas above however so that your faith brings your questioning closer to God.

<u>Bruce's Legacy on Thriving:</u>

Faith was extremely important to Bruce, even before he started his battle against cancer and other serious illnesses. He realized that faith is the only true path to Hope. This hope would provide comfort and encouragement to him with the knowledge that all of his suffering was only temporary. While this Hope was welcome because his pain would be released in the next life, his faith was the foundation to make sure others would similarly seek the light in faith.

<u>Foundation in Scripture:</u>

"Now faith is confidence in what we hope for and assurance about what we do not see. This is what the ancients were commended for." (Hebrews 11:1-2, NIV)

<u>My Notes / Action Plan:</u>

2. Research

<u>Key to Thriving:</u>

Trust but verify. Trust your doctor but get additional opinions. Consider information from an article by a medical center at greater credit than an opinion article. Be mindful of what you read online. Conduct your own research and then discuss your findings with your doctor. Have an open and honest conversation with your doctor regarding the benefits, potential side effects, and other information that you have learned in your research.

<u>Bruce's Legacy on Thriving:</u>

Hours. Probably more like days. Perhaps even a week or so. That's the amount of time that Bruce spent on the computer researching his illnesses. It's not that he didn't trust the doctors, it's just that he wanted to have as much information as possible so that he and Donna could make an informed decision. No, that's not quite it: he NEEDED to have as much information as possible to make the decision.

<u>Foundation in Scripture:</u>

"The simple believe anything, but the prudent give thought to their steps." (Proverbs 14:15, NIV)

<u>My Notes / Action Plan:</u>

3. Intercessory Prayer

<u>Key to Thriving:</u>
   This life is a journey, one that we do not traverse alone. We have all built relationships, some intimate, some close, and some mere acquaintances. When we go through struggles, so do those that walk beside us during the journey. We will need to tap into their strength during our struggles so that we can continue fighting when we are down and out.
   But we also need to pray for comfort for our support structure. We need to pray that God will bolster them so that they can provide exactly what we need, when we need it during our struggle.

<u>Bruce's Legacy on Thriving:</u>
   In the midst of his struggle while facing prostate cancer, Bruce spent time praying for his family: his wife, his sons, his grandchildren, his mother, his brother, his brother-in-law, his sisters-in-law, and all sorts of nieces, nephews, aunts, and uncles. He was well aware that his struggle would have both a short term and long term effect on their lives. His desire was to intercede on their behalf and ask that God would provide them comfort, strength, and encouragement during this struggle. It is not difficult to assume that Bruce also prayed the same for his close friends as well.

<u>Foundation in Scripture:</u>
   "In the same way, the Spirit helps us in our weakness. We do not know what we ought to pray for, but the Spirit himself intercedes for us through wordless groans." (Romans 8:26, NIV)
   "The prayer of a righteous person is powerful and effective." (James 5:16b, NIV)

<u>My Notes / Action Plan:</u>

4. Power of Music

Key to Thriving:

Music is a huge part of our lives; the integration of digital music players and radio applications on our mobile phones have made it possible for us to listen to music whenever and wherever we desire to listen. In our society, even if we don't want to listen to music, it is very difficult to not hear music on the radio, television, etc. Most stores even have music playing in the background.

Music is important because it speaks to us: It speaks to us if we are going through heartache, if we are grieving, even if we are happy. Finding music and lyrics that speak to us during life's struggles gives us the strength to move forward and fight. When you find songs that help, save them, and listen to them often.

Bruce's Legacy on Thriving:

When presented a choice between hymns and modern worship songs, Bruce preferred hymns. He found hymns to be constant songs sung during worship services throughout the majority of his life. "How Great Thou Art" was his favorite hymn. He even asked for the song to be sung during his memorial service. That being said, he wasn't necessarily a big singer during the service, but he did appreciate the lyrics of the hymns. There are many times that he would research the lyrics and find solace in the words and the message that was communicated.

Foundation in Scripture:

"I will praise God's name in song and glorify him with thanksgiving." (Psalms 69:30, NIV)

My Notes / Action Plan:

5. Battle Plan

Key to Thriving:

When faced with insurmountable odds, such as a cancer diagnosis, the path forward is to take it one step at a time. To be most effective, it is important to create a plan based upon the ultimate goal and then determine the steps required to get to the destination. Create a plan of attack, with multiple contingencies for when things go awry. Share the plan with your loved ones. Hold yourself accountable to the plan.

Bruce's Legacy on Thriving:

"Hope is not a strategy". This simple phrase was no doubt drilled into Bruce by the military, starting from basic training until he retired as a general. Simple saying, but powerful. Bruce definitely took it to task throughout his life, his career, his work with the church, and yes, even his family. Not only did he plan for the fight, but he also planned for his untimely exit from this earth. His two "what to do if I die" binders were the most intense planning that the funeral director had ever seen, read, or been given.

Foundation in Scripture:

"Trust in the Lord with all your heart and lean not on your own understanding; in all your ways submit to him, and he will make your paths straight" (Proverbs 3:5-6, NIV)

"Commit to the Lord whatever you do, and he will establish your plans." (Proverbs 16:3, NIV)

My Notes / Action Plan:

6. Communicate

Key to Thriving:

The "unofficial" definition of the word "assume" is important to fully understand in all relationships, including those between someone going through intense struggles and their support network. When someone assumes, they "make an xxx out of you and me".

Assuming is thus not productive to the healing, comfort, and encouragement necessary to overcome cancer or any illness. Patients: don't assume; communicate your needs verbally to your support team. Caregivers: Don't assume; if the patient isn't talking, ask questions.

For both the patient and caregiver: don't assume that you understand the other person, or even that communication has actually happened. Ask for confirmation.

Bruce's Legacy on Thriving:

Unfortunately, this is another episode where Bruce's example was the opposite of how to thrive. Quoting from his journal when he found out it was prostate cancer: "Everyone in the car was silent. No one talked about it much...However I had a desire to talk about it...". The lesson? Don't be like Bruce. Talk about it. In other words: Communicate.

Foundation in Scripture:

"For who knows a person's thoughts except their own spirit within them?" (1 Corinthians 2:11a, NIV)

My Notes / Action Plan:

7. Seek Support

<u>Key to Thriving:</u>

Humans tend to try to be self-sufficient, including when we go through significant struggles. In addition, our society has turned seeking help from others into a sign of weakness. So we don't; we often suffer in silence.

The wars and conflicts of the late 20th and early 21st centuries have provided thousands of examples of the dangers of military members keeping feelings and emotions suppressed. The repercussions of this mentality are receiving widespread attention because many of our military are suffering. First responders such as police, firemen & women, paramedics, medical personnel, and many others are also suffering as well.

It is becoming clear that we are not made this way; we are made to interact with other human beings. Sharing with each other to build each other up is wired into our DNA.

Whatever you are dealing with, it is possible to find support, either from in-person groups or online groups. The Internet is wonderful in this situation with the plethora of support options available to everyone.

<u>Bruce's Legacy on Thriving:</u>

Bruce recognized that despite all his best efforts, he was human, and not perfect. He would be the first one to acknowledge failures. For this item specifically, Bruce would have admitted that he should have done a better job of finding and attending support groups. Whether it was a group for prostate cancer, thyroid cancer, or skin cancer, if he had wanted to, he could have found a support group to lean on during his struggle.

Learn from his missteps: find a support group and attend. Today.

<u>Foundation in Scripture:</u>

"Though one may be overpowered, two can defend themselves. A cord of three strands is not quickly broken." (Ecclesiastes 4:12, NIV)

"And let us consider how we may spur one another on towards love and good deeds, not giving up meeting together, as some are in the habit of doing, but encouraging one another-and all the more as you see the Day approaching." (Hebrews 10:24-25, NIV)

My Notes / Action Plan:

8. Connecting

<u>Key to Thriving:</u>
There is power in discovering others that either have gone through, or are currently going through, similar situations and struggles. Although my heart was in the right place, I could not understand what Bruce was going through as he faced prostate cancer, thyroid issues, and skin cancer. I didn't know how he was feeling and thus didn't know what to say to ease his struggle. I didn't know the right words.

But the survivors that Bruce connected with did know the right words to say. They did know what he was going through and what he needed to hear. Words matter, and they knew the right words. This connection is vital in order to thrive during life's struggles.

<u>Bruce's Legacy on Thriving:</u>
Bruce knew that his battle was not unique; many others had been diagnosed with prostate cancer before him and many others would be diagnosed after Bruce's struggle. He also knew that there was power in connecting with other survivors. Hearing that someone else is around today after having successfully fought cancer will provide encouragement to those who are without hope. Although he didn't attend many support groups, he did actively seek out neighbors and men at church that had survived prostate cancer to learn from their experiences.

<u>Foundation in Scripture:</u>
"Therefore encourage one another and build each other up, just as in fact you are doing." (1 Thessalonians 5:11, NIV)

<u>My Notes / Action Plan:</u>

9. Brotherhood/Sisterhood

Key to Thriving:

Whatever battle you are facing, you are absolutely, positively not going it alone. Others have gone through similar struggles, have come out on the other side, and are available for support and encouragement.

Whereas the previous key was focused on the act, or the search for others going through similar struggles, this key speaks to the necessity for an ongoing relationship between yourself and that person.

It is important to find someone (or multiple people) that can provide the support that is necessary for your journey through the struggle of prostate cancer or other illnesses. Find yourself someone who either has been in the foxhole or will join you in the foxhole during this struggle. Find yourself a battle buddy. Someone who will be there in the middle of the night to answer your phone call. Someone who will meet you for coffee or lunch because you need to vent about your struggle.

Bruce's Legacy on Thriving:

Bruce wore his blue wrist band everywhere *while* he was going through treatment for prostate cancer in order to generate conversations with men who had survived prostate cancer. He wore his blue wrist band *after* he had successfully beaten prostate cancer in order to generate conversations with men who were going through prostate cancer. He told several stories of meeting strangers while shopping or while dining in restaurants simply because the other person saw the blue band on Dad's wrist.

His goal through all this? Create bonds with men to strengthen each other while they were, quite literally, fighting for their lives.

Foundation in Scripture:

"Carry each other's burdens, and in this way you will fufill the law of Christ." (Galatians 6:2, NIV)

"When Job's three friends, Eliphaz the Temanite, Bildad the Shuhite and Zophar the Naamathite, heard about all the troubles that had come upon him, they set out from their homes and met together by agreement to go and sympathize with him and comfort him." (Job 2:11, NIV)

My Notes / Action Plan:

10. Anchor

<u>Key to Thriving:</u>

Identify something that you can cling to when the going gets rough. If you're a believer, then your anchor should be nothing other than Jesus Christ.

If you're not a believer, find something that gives you hope. Something that you can focus on in the trough of the waves. Your anchor might be your family. Your anchor might be your battle buddy. Your anchor might be gardening or some other hobby. Ultimately, if you search long enough, it is our prayer that your search will bring you to faith in Jesus Christ.

<u>Bruce's Legacy on Thriving:</u>

There is no dispute as to what Bruce's anchor was: His faith in Jesus Christ. His faith was instrumental throughout his adult life. His faith was his internal anchor: he spent countless hours throughout this life in the study of the Bible to grow his faith. His faith was an external anchor: He was an active member of churches wherever he lived: Springfield, IL, Oregon, IL, and Bonita Springs, FL.

<u>Foundation in Scripture:</u>

"We have this hope as an anchor for the soul, firm and secure. It enters the inner sanctuary behind the curtain." (Hebrews 6:19, NIV)

"Consequently, faith comes from hearing the message, and the message is heard through the word about Christ." (Romans 10:17, NIV)

<u>My Notes / Action Plan:</u>

11. Outward Focus

Key to Thriving:

Step outside of yourself. Take a break from focusing on the trials and struggles that you are facing. Realize that others are going through struggles as well. Sometimes their struggles may be more severe than your own. Help them. You'll be surprised that by focusing on others, you often will cease focusing on yourself and consequently, your perspective and mental attitude improves.

Bruce's Legacy on Thriving:

No one would have faulted Bruce if he had given up, stayed in the house, and watched TV or played video games all day. At points in his life, Bruce was fighting prostate cancer, issues with his thyroid, skin cancer, and a fairly significant bicycle accident.

But he didn't stay on the couch. He went outside his house and served his community. He put countless hours volunteering at his church, the local VFW, at a Christian youth camp in Texas, and volunteered at local homeless shelters. Bruce realized that helping others was critical to his path forward. He maintained his relationships not only for his own sake, but for the sake of those others.

Foundation in Scripture:

"Therefore we do not lose heart. Though outwardly we are wasting away, yet inwardly we are being renewed day by day. For our light and momentary troubles are achieving for us an eternal glory that far outweighs them all. So we fix our eyes not on what is seen, but on what is unseen, since what is seen is temporary, but what is unseen is eternal." (2 Corinthians 4:16-18, NIV)

My Notes / Action Plan:

12. Get out of Bed

Key to Thriving:

The hardest step to healing, to improving your struggle, is the first step, which is the step out from the bed. Sure, there is time for withdrawal and sleeping all day. But that's not every day. Nor is it even most days.

If you want to thrive, you first have to get out of bed. You must make the choice every day to get out of bed.

The second choice you must make then is to focus on the good of the situation and not the bad. Find a positive, no matter how small of a detail it is compared to your struggle. Focus on the small step forward, not the large leap backward.

Be a beacon to others that they may see your positive attitude when you are in the midst of struggles.

Bruce's Legacy on Thriving:

At times during his struggles, Bruce was in a tremendous amount of pain. Whether it was from the prostate cancer, the growths around his thyroid, skin cancer treatments, recovery from the bicycle accident, and the hernia issue, Bruce endured a lot of physical pain.

But despite the pain, Bruce got up each morning and lived his life to be a blessing and encouragement to others. All of these volunteer efforts required physical exertions, from a body that was failing him.

Despite all of his failing health, he believed that there were others who didn't have it as good as him. So he gave of his time to make their lives better.

Foundation in Scripture:

"Even youths grow tired and weary, and young men stumble and fall; but those who hope in the LORD will renew their strength. They will soar on wings like eagles; they will run and not grow weary, they will walk and not be faint." (Isaiah 40:30-31, NIV)

"You are the light of the world. A town built on a hill cannot be hidden. Neither do people light a lamp and put it under a bowl. Instead they put it on its stand, and it gives light to everyone in the house. In the same way, let your light shine before others, that they may see your good deeds and glorify your Father in heaven. (Matthew 5:14-16, NIV)

"But you, Lord, do not be far from me. You are my strength; come quickly to help me." (Psalm 22:19, NIV)

"The Sovereign Lord is my strength; he makes my feet like the feet of a deer, he enables me to tread on the heights." (Habakkuk 3:19, NIV)

My Notes / Action Plan:

13. Ever Forward

<u>Key to Thriving:</u>

You will get knocked down during your struggle. Guaranteed. None of us are immune from being beaten down by life during our journey on this planet. If you are reading this book, then you already know that it is critical to get back up and get back into the fight. That takes courage.

But it takes just as much courage to **keep** moving forward. In fact, it might even take more courage to continue moving forward, moving towards the fight. That is just as critical to your journey. You must make the choice to move forward.

<u>Bruce's Legacy on Thriving:</u>

After his bicycle crash, Bruce got back onto the bicycle as soon as possible. The skeptic might say that the only reason he got back up was to dispel any fear that he might have concerning biking. If this was the case, then Bruce would have gotten back on the bicycle, biked a mile or so, and called it quits. But this wasn't the case. Bruce got back on the bike, moved forward, and resumed biking 10, 15, 20+ miles.

<u>Foundation in Scripture:</u>

"He gives strength to the weary and increases the power of the weak." (Isaiah 40:29, NIV)

"So do not fear, for I am with you; do not be dismayed, for I am your God. I will strengthen you and help you; I will uphold you with my righteous right hand." (Isaiah 41:10, NIV)

<u>My Notes / Action Plan:</u>

14. Making Memories

Key to Thriving:

Despite all his efforts, all of his prayers, all of his trips to doctors, and all of his surgeries, Bruce knew that he wasn't going to be around forever. He didn't know when he would leave this earth, but he knew that sooner or later, Death would come knocking at his door. Throughout his life he wanted to make sure that his family, friends, and acquaintances would remember him.

None of us are guaranteed to live forever. There will come a time, that despite all of our efforts, we will pass on from this earth. When we do, all that will remain of us will be memories in those around us. We are wholly responsible to ensure that we create positive gatherings, experiences, or conversations that create a memory for those that remain.

How are you making memories?

Bruce's Legacy on Thriving:

This is another area of his life that troubled Bruce. On the one hand he was driven to pursue excellence at his work for the National Guard and the Illinois State Police. But on the other hand, he understood the need to focus on his family and create memories with them that would last a lifetime. Bruce mentioned this struggle a couple of times in his journal.

But in reality, he didn't need to worry because there were plenty of times where memories were made as a family and with friends. We were fortunate enough to go on a couple of vacations every year as a family. Just one example that I will never forget was our van vacation to California: trying to camp overnight in Needles, California, touring the Spruce Goose, and pulling over to the side of the road when my brother got sick are all memories that are fondly seared in my memory.

Foundation in Scripture:

"So I hated life, because the work that is done under the sun was grievous to me. All of it is meaningless, a chasing after the wind. I hated all the things I had toiled for under the sun, because I must leave them to the one who comes after me. And who knows whether that person will be wise or foolish? Yet they will have control over all the fruit of my toil into which I have poured my effort and skill under the sun. This too is meaningless. So my heart began to despair over all my toilsome labor under the sun. For a person may labor with wisdom, knowledge and skill, and then they must leave all they own to another who has not toiled for it. This too is meaningless and a great misfortune. What do people get for all the toil and anxious striving with which they labor under the sun? All their days their work is grief and pain; even at night their minds do not rest. This too is meaningless.

A person can do nothing better than to eat and drink and find satisfaction in their own toil. This too, I see, is from the hand of God, for without him, who can eat or find enjoyment? To the person who pleases him, God gives wisdom, knowledge and happiness, but to the sinner he gives the task of gathering and storing up wealth to hand it over to the one who pleases God. This too is meaningless, a chasing after the wind." (Ecclesiastes 2:17-26, NIV)

My Notes / Action Plan:

15. Stubbornness

Quick: What is one thing that your parents instilled in you from a young age? Answer: To play nice with others. One example of that is to see an argument or area of conflict from the other person's point of view. Be willing to compromise.

With apologies to parents everywhere, I am going to give you permission to be stubborn while on your journey. Be resolute in the following: I will not let this disease negatively affect who I am and my purpose in life. Too tired to get out of the house and spend time with friends? Be stubborn and make the choice to get out of the house and into the world.

Bruce's Legacy on Thriving:

Finding an example of this from Bruce's life isn't difficult; the challenge is to narrow down the examples to one for the purpose of helping others thrive. Bruce was old school: whenever he felt like he had been slighted or received less than satisfactory service, he did what many Baby Boomers used to do; he wrote a letter. We have dozens of letters that he wrote to corporations such as hotel chains, airlines, and even restaurants. There was just something about him that couldn't let the issue slide and move on with his day. Nope. He was stubborn and he was compelled to seek what he believed was justice.

Foundation in Scripture:

"He will make your righteous reward shine like the dawn, your vindication like the noonday sun." (Psalm 37:6, NIV)

"Therefore, my dear brothers and sisters, stand firm. Let nothing move you. Always give yourselves fully to the work of the Lord, because you know that your labor in the Lord is not in vain." (1 Corinthians 15:58, NIV)

My Notes / Action Plan:

16. Journaling

<u>Key to Thriving:</u>

Record your journey for yourself so that when you are on the other side, you can go back and realize the blessings that you received during the struggles. Record your journey for others so that they may be blessed by seeing your blessings.

Remember: You are not in this struggle alone. You have people right now today that are invested in your health and wellness during your struggle. There will be people that you haven't even met yet who could benefit from your thoughts during your struggle.

<u>Bruce's Legacy on Thriving:</u>

Bruce's journal was 77 pages in standard word processing style. Our family is so grateful that he took time to document his experience throughout his struggle. We are grateful to be able to learn and understand what he was thinking and his emotional state. We are saddened however that we are only now able to read his journals, after he is gone. Don't be like Bruce. Journal, but share it with those around you.

Or don't share it. Perhaps you need to share ugly thoughts that you don't want others to hear. This is perfectly acceptable. If you only write with a mind towards others, you may not be able to express all of the feelings that you need to express. Keep a journal of your struggles and then consider supplementing it with writings to those you love.

There are many online options for journaling. One of the most popular is a site called Caring Bridge (www.caringbridge.org), which permits the patient or caregiver to communicate updates to loved ones throughout periods of illness.

<u>Foundation in Scripture:</u>

"Let this be written for a future generation, that a people not yet created may praise the Lord." (Psalm 102:18, NIV)

"Therefore encourage one another and build each other up, just as in fact you are doing." (1 Thessalonians 5:11, NIV)

"We have different gifts, according to the grace given to each of us. If your gift is prophesying, then prophesy in accordance with your faith; if it is serving, then serve; if it is teaching, then teach; if it is to encourage, then give encouragement; if it is giving, then give generously; if it is to lead, do it diligently; if it is to show mercy, do it cheerfully." (Romans 12:6-8, NIV)

My Notes / Action Plan:

17. Hobbies

<u>Key to Thriving:</u>
     The struggle that you are going through is an all-consuming monster. It will take everything you have if you let the monster run loose through your life. You need a distraction from time to time. Does the monster require your focused attention so that you can battle it effectively? Absolutely. But at the same time, your mental health and sanity need a break. Find a constructive hobby. Something that will take your mind off your struggle, if just for a few minutes every day.

<u>Bruce's Legacy on Thriving:</u>
     Bruce had his share of hobbies. His passion for bicycling has been well documented in this book. But he also was an avid (and gifted) woodworker. Along the way he collected baseball cards to connect with his sons. He was a firearms enthusiast, even going so far as to load his own ammunition. He and Donna took up a hobby called Volksmarching which is basically walking a 10k in a beautiful locale. Later in life he enjoyed playing card games with family and friends. He realized that hobbies were important because they helped him mentally escape from his struggle.

<u>Foundation in Scripture:</u>
     "Do not let your hearts be troubled. You believe in God; believe also in me." (John 14:1, NIV)
     "Finally, brothers and sisters, whatever is true, whatever is noble, whatever is right, whatever is pure, whatever is lovely, whatever is admirable - if anything is excellent or praiseworthy - think about such things. Whatever you have learned or received or heard from me, or seen in me-put into practice. And the God of peace will be with you." (Philippians 4:8-9, NIV)

<u>My Notes / Action Plan:</u>

18. Perseverance

<u>Key to Thriving:</u>

The journey will be rough. Your journey will be wholly unique to you. No one else will completely understand your struggles. Your plan will be to make it to the end of the struggle, when the disease has been beaten. And that will be a glorious day when the struggle is over.

But appreciate the journey. Learn from your struggles. Use what you learned to become a better person. Become a better encourager to others as they are in the midst of their own journey. There is a saying that is in danger of becoming a cliche, which is a shame because the saying is accurate. The saying reminds us to be nice to everyone because we don't know what they are dealing with in their life and whether they are persevering.

Remember: life is during the journey, not at the end. There are still beautiful moments to enjoy along the road. If you spend all your time wishing for the end of something when it gets there, you will look back and see that you missed a lot in looking too far ahead.

<u>Bruce's Legacy on Thriving:</u>

Bruce realized that "this too shall pass". Throughout all his issues, Bruce continued to persevere. Each time he received bad news from a doctor, there was a brief period where he was down and out, but it was only for a short while. After he was done being mad, he got back into the fight and continued onward during the struggle.

He persevered so that he could continue with his mission of being a blessing to others. He persevered so that others could learn from his journey. His journal, the basis for this book, is a testament to Dad's legacy on thriving through his perseverance.

<u>Foundation in Scripture:</u>

"Consider it pure joy, my brothers and sisters, whenever you face trails of many kinds, because you know that the testing of your faith produces perseverance. Let perseverance finish its work so that you may be mature and complete, not lacking anything." (James 1:2-4, NIV)

"Therefore, since we have been justified through faith, we have peace with God through our Lord Jesus Christ, through whom we have gained access by faith into this grace in which we now stand. And we boast in the hope of the glory of God. Not only so, but we also glory in our sufferings, because we know that suffering produces perseverance; perseverance, character; and character, hope." (Romans 5:1-4, NIV)

My Notes / Action Plan:

19. Get Up and Fight

Key to Thriving:

More specifically, get up and get back in the fight when you are knocked down. Make no mistake: If you are reading this book then you're likely in the thick of it and the disease will knock you down. Possibly often. Perhaps even daily. There will be days when you don't want even get out of bed because the disease has a strong hold over your body.

Just like Bruce couldn't control the amount of bad news he was getting, we cannot control when we get knocked down. But we can control whether we get up and get back into the fight.

Today may be the day when you are able to bless the life of a friend or a stranger when you get out of bed.

Bruce's Legacy on Thriving:

There were several entries in Bruce's journal where he learned of bad news from his doctor during successive days. For example: On December 15, 2011, Bruce began having problem with a hernia. Then on the 16th he began losing sight in his right eye. Those would be devastating and no one would blame Bruce if he adopted a "Woe is Me" mentality and withdrew from society. But he got up on the 17th and got back into the fight.

Foundation in Scripture:

"We put no stumbling block in anyone's path, so that our ministry will not be discredited. Rather, as servants of God we commend ourselves in every way: in great endurance; in troubles, hardships and distresses; in beatings, imprisonments and riots; in hard work, sleepless nights and hunger; in purity, understanding, patience and kindness; in the Holy Spirit and in sincere love; in truthful speech and in the power of God; with weapons of righteousness in the right hand and in the left; through glory and dishonor, bad report and good report; genuine, yet regarded as impostors; known, yet regarded as unknown; dying, and yet we live on; beaten and not yet killed; sorrowful, yet always rejoicing; poor, yet making many rich; having nothing, and yet possessing everything." (2 Corinthians 6:3-10, NIV)

"I have fought the good fight, I have finished the race, I have kept the faith. Now there is in store for me the crown of righteousness, which the Lord, the righteous Judge, will award to me on that day — and not only to me, but also to all who have longed for his appearing." (2 Timothy 4:7-8, NIV)

My Notes / Action Plan:

20. Relationships

<u>Key to Thriving:</u>

The struggle is yours but also not yours. Focus on spending time with others. Visit with existing friends. Create new relationships. Remember: you are an example of what thriving looks like to those who are familiar with your struggle. Their lives will be blessed by the relationship with you.

Also remember that you're not alone; share your journey with others. Don't be afraid to tell others how you're feeling. You never know when someone will pass nuggets of wisdom to you.

Consider counseling, someone who you can share your entire journey, everything, in a safe environment. They are paid to hear what you say but you don't have to worry how it will impact your relationship with that person.

<u>Bruce's Legacy on Thriving:</u>

No matter the bad news, no matter how he was feeling, Bruce continued to spend time with others: his friends, he spent time socializing with people at the local VFW and at church, he spent time getting to know new people and turning acquaintances into friends. Bruce realized that spending time with friends was a distraction from the realities of struggling with diseases, which improved his journey.

But don't feel like you have to spend ALL of your time with other people. You will need to have times of rest and respite. There were dozens, if not hundreds, of times when Bruce could be found taking a nap in his recliner with a newspaper over his head separating him from the outside world.

<u>Foundation in Scripture:</u>

"One who has unreliable friends soon comes to ruin, but there is a friend who sticks closer than a brother." (Proverbs 18:24, NIV. This verse seems to be the basis for the song, "God Really Loves Us", by Crowder and Dante Bowe. Search for the lyrics on your Internet browser for a blessed description of the relationship God wants with us.)

"Love must be sincere. Hate what is evil; cling to what is good. Be devoted to one another in love. Honor one another above yourselves. Never be lacking in zeal, but keep your spiritual fervor, serving the Lord. Be joyful in hope, patient in affliction, faithful in prayer. Share with the Lord's people who are in need. Practice hospitality." (Romans 12:9-13, NIV)

"A new command I give you: Love one another. As I have loved you, so you must love one another. By this everyone will know that you are my disciples, if you love one another." (John 13, 34, NIV)

My Notes / Action Plan:

21. Cling to Hope

<u>Key to Thriving:</u>

Focus on the positive. Fill your minds with positive thoughts. Embrace the feeling that you will make it through the struggle, one way or another.

This world can be a dark place, especially if you are fighting a life-altering or potentially life-ending disease. But we cannot give in to the darkness and despair that are common today.

There is hope on the other side; you've just got to make it through the struggles to get there. It's going to be a journey and all we can do is to take it one step at a time, one day at a time.

Without hope we have nothing to strive for or focus on during the darkest of days.

<u>Bruce's Legacy on Thriving:</u>

Bruce had the hope that no matter how the diseases tried to make his life difficult, if not to end it, his ultimate hope was passing from this life to the next.

It was Bruce's desire that all should come to faith in Jesus Christ so that this life is not the end. This is the ultimate hope we have on this earth.

Dad would want part of his legacy to be that all who are reading his journal would eventually join him in heaven. This was a significant factor in Bruce's ability to face his journey with courage, to finish the fight.

<u>Foundation in Scripture:</u>

"Not only so, but we also glory in our sufferings, because we know that suffering produces perseverance; perseverance, character; and character, hope. And hope does not put us to shame, because God's love has been poured out into our hearts through the Holy Spirit, who has been given to us. You see, at just the right time, when we were still powerless, Christ died for the ungodly. Very rarely will anyone die for a righteous person, though for a good person someone might possibly dare to die. But God demonstrates his own love for us in this: While we were still sinners, Christ died for us. Since we have now been justified by his blood, how much more shall we be saved from God's wrath through him! For if, while we were God's enemies, we were reconciled to him through the death of his Son, how much more, having been reconciled, shall we be saved through his life! Not only is this so, but we also boast in God through our Lord Jesus Christ, through whom we have now received reconciliation." (Romans 5:3-11, NIV)

"I have fought the good fight, I have finished the race, I have kept the faith." (2 Timothy 4:7, NIV)

My Notes / Action Plan:

Appendices

Appendix A: Obituary

Bruce W. VanderKolk 3/16/1945 - 2/18/2018 Bonita Springs, FL—
Bruce W. VanderKolk, 72, of Bonita Springs, FL and formerly of
Oregon, IL, died Sunday, February 18, 2018. He was born March 16,
1945 in Allegan, MI, the son of Wiley and Violet VanderKolk. He
married Donna Sue Townsend in 1968.

Mr. VanderKolk graduated from Hopkins High School in 1963 and
from Michigan State University in 1967. He received his Masters
degree in 1977 from the University of Illinois at Chicago. While at
Michigan State University he was a member of the ROTC program
and upon graduation he was commissioned a Second Lieutenant. He
served in the active Army from 1967-1969 and was a Vietnam
veteran. Upon leaving the active Army in 1969, he remained in the
Reserve Components and retired in 1994 from the Illinois National
Guard as a Brigadier General. He received the Legion of Merit, Bronze
Star, Meritorious Service Medal with two oak leaf clusters and Army
Commendation Medal with one oak leaf cluster.

After leaving the active Army, he joined the Illinois State Police in
1969 and served in a variety of positions, retiring in 2001 as the
Commander of the Forensic Sciences Command. He was an Emeritus
member of the American Society of Crime Laboratory Directors and
Midwestern Association of Forensic Scientists.

He was a member of Anchor Christian Church in Bonita Springs,
FL where he and his wife lived. He was a prior member of Southside
Christian Church in Springfield, IL. While living in Oregon, IL, he
attended the Oregon Church of God. He was a member of Oregon VFW
Post 8739 and Oregon American Legion Post 97.

Mr. VanderKolk is survived by his loving wife of 49 years, Donna
Sue; his sons, Roger VanderKolk of Woodbury, MN, and James (Shelia)
VanderKolk of Oregon, IL; and seven cherished grandchildren, Ethan,
Corey, Sean, Matthew, Nadia, Caelyn and Madilyn.

A funeral service will be held Thursday, February 22, 2018 at

11:00 a.m. at Anchor Christian Church, Bonita Springs. Visitation for family and friends will take place at the church from 10:00 a.m. until the time of the service. A celebration of life service will be held Thursday, March 1, 2018 at 5:00 p.m. at the South Side Christian Church, 2600 S MacArthur Blvd., Springfield, IL. Graveside services with Military Honors will take place Saturday, March 3, 2018 at 1:00 p.m. at Maplewood Cemetery in Hopkins, MI. In lieu of flowers, the family suggests that memorial contributions be made to the Anchor Christian Church Building Fund, 11651 E Terry Street, Bonita Springs, FL 34135.

Appendix B: Bruce Wiley VanderKolk Curriculum Vitae

Education
- Michigan State University, B.S. Police Administration w/ emphasis in Forensic Science 1967
- University Illinois at Chicago, MS, Criminalistics, 1977
- Command and General Staff Course, Military 1982

Forensic Science/ManagementExperience
- October 1995 - June 2001: (Retired) Commander, IL State Police, Forensic Sciences Command
- January 1978 - October 1995: Bureau Chief, IL State Police, Bureau of Forensic Sciences
- October 1977 - December 1977: Assistant Bureau Chief, IL Dept. Law Enforcement, Springfield
- February 1973 - September 1977: Laboratory Director, IL Dept. Law Enforcement, Maywood
- September 1970 - January 1973: Laboratory Director, IL Dept. Law Enforcement, Rock Island
- October 1969 - August 1970: Drug Chemist, IL Dept. Law Enforcement, Joliet

Forensic Science/Management Assigned Responsibilities

Commander: Served as Commander of the Forensic Sciences Command, Illinois State Police, which consisted of eight regional forensic science laboratories and a Research and Development laboratory, consisting of a total staff of 468. Oversaw and coordinated the prompt, accurate and appropriate delivery of laboratory analyses and polygraph examinations involving 110,000 criminal cases in support of criminal justice agencies within Illinois. Additionally, the States DNA Convicted Sexual Assault data base was implemented within the Forensic Sciences Command.

NOTE: During the early 90s, an agreement was reached between the City of Chicago and the Governor of Illinois in which the Chicago Police Department Crime Laboratory Function would be transferred to the Illinois State Police. I was responsible for managing the merger which consisted of determining which Chicago Police Department employees would be transferred, hiring the management staff, establishing systems to ensure the prompt and accurate analysis of approximately an additional 55,000 cases, hiring approximately an additional 150 new forensic scientists and providing appropriate training, and implementing a laboratory management information system to track evidence, provide reports, statistical data and online capabilities with the Cook County States Attorneys Office. In July 1996 the transfer was completed and one year later the laboratory received national accreditation by the American Society of Crime Laboratory Directors-Laboratory Accreditation Board.

Bureau Chief: Served as Bureau Chief of the Bureau of Forensic Sciences, Illinois State Police, which consisted of seven regional forensic science laboratories and a Research and Development laboratory, consisting of a total staff of approximately 310. Oversaw and coordinated the prompt, accurate and appropriate delivery of laboratory analyses and polygraph examinations in support of criminal justice agencies within Illinois. During this period the nations first Training and Applications Laboratory was established to train new forensic scientists plus the nations first formalize Quality Assurance Program was implemented. These two areas were important in that a sound training program was established to ensure well-trained forensic scientists were placed in the laboratories and the Quality Assurance program monitored statewide the accuracy, timeliness and completeness of forensic analyses.

NOTE: In 1985, the State's Forensic Toxicology program operating under the control of the Department of Public Health was transferred to the Illinois State Police by direction of the Governor due to improper management and analytical practices. I managed the transfer and because of issues determined that none of the current employees would be accepted. The function was relocated from the Chicago area to Springfield and all new staff were hired, facilities obtained, and policies/protocols developed.

Assistant Bureau Chief: Responsible to the bureau chief for administering support functions for several forensic laboratories, including, but not limited to, budget preparation, administrative transactions, policy/procedural development, training and quality assurance issues.

Laboratory Director - Maywood: Served as the laboratory director for the Maywood Forensic Science Laboratory. Responsible for providing forensic science services to the greater metropolitan Chicago area, excluding the City of Chicago. Directed the activities of several forensic science disciplines and administrative functions.

Laboratory Director - Rock Island: Served as the laboratory director for the Rock Island Forensic Science Laboratory. Responsible for providing forensic science services to the northwestern portion of Illinois. Directed the activities of forensic science disciplines, polygraph and crime scene investigation.

Crime Laboratory Analyst: Conducted forensic examinations in the areas of drug chemistry, arson and blood alcohol. Responsible for the interpretation and reporting of results of analyses to user agencies and subsequent court testimony.

Teaching: 1971 to 1972 - Instructor in forensic science/crime scene investigation at Blackhawk College.

Military Assignments

Numerous military assignments from 1967 to 1994, to include active duty in Vietnam; retired August 28, 1994, as Brigadier General, Illinois Army National Guard. During 27 years of military service, 15 years were involved as a commander of different units. These included company, battalion and brigade levels, plus command of the Illinois Military Academy. Also served as principle staff officer at battalion and brigade levels.

Professional Occupation Since Retiring From The Illinois State Police
April 2010 to December 2010

Served as the Executive Administrator for South Side Christian Church, Springfield, Illinois. After the Senior Minister left his position,

I was asked to oversee the ministerial and support staff of the church. Responsible for coordinating the staff at two campuses and overseeing the day to day operations of the church. Served as the liaison between the staff and the Board of Elders.

August 30, 2004 to December 31, 2006

Served as the Assimilating/Equipping Ministry Director for South Side Christian Church, Springfield, Illinois

Responsible for developing processes to involve church attendees in serving as a volunteer in one of the many volunteer positions; training leaders of volunteers to help improve their skills in recruiting, retaining and proper placement of volunteers; one of five members serving on the Vision Planning Team developing and overseeing the strategy planning process for the church.

August 1, 2001 to August 29, 2004

Served as the Church Administrator for South Side Christian Church, Springfield, Illinois. I was hired as the first church administrator and given responsibilities for supervising all of the support staff, managing the facilities, establishing policies and procedures, overseeing the budget and preparation of new fiscal year budgets (approximately 1.2 m), recruiting and assigning volunteers, and working on special projects either for the Senior Minister or Board of Elders.

Professional Organizations
- American Society of Crime Laboratory Directors (Served on legislative/strategic planning committee and Board of Directors), Emeritus Member
- Midwestern Association of Forensic Sciences, Charter Member, President, Secretary, Treasurer, Newsletter Editor, Emeritus Member
- Illinois Association of Identification
- National Guard Association of Illinois
- National Guard Association of United States
- Reserve Officers Association

- American Legion Post 97, Oregon, IL
- VFW Post 8739, Oregon, IL, Life Member

Professional Activities

- Assisted as a consultant to Bianchi Consulting, Ltd., reviewing selected areas of the New York Police Department Forensic Laboratory, March 2008.
- Served in various leadership training capacities to the following: Maritime Christian College in Prince Edward Island, Restoration House in New Hampshire, Anchor Christian Church in Bonita Springs Florida.
- Served on the Advisory Board to The Independent Investigator for the Houston Police Department Crime Laboratory and Property Room, April 2005 to June 2007.
- Trainer and Instructor for the Illinois Regional Institute for Community Policing on DNA: Evidence Identification, Collection, & Preservation for Law Enforcement, 2005, 2006
- Served as Lead Auditor & Human Resources Auditor, City of Phoenix, City Auditor Department, performing a Police Crime Laboratory Audit of the Phoenix Police Department, 2003-2004.
- On an informal basis prepared a Proposal for Forensic Services for Chief Terrance Gainer, Metropolitan Police Department, District of Columbia
- Served on a team in the late 1990s as a consultant to the New York Police Department Crime Laboratory to help prepare the laboratory for national accreditation by the ASCLD-LAB.
- Member, National Center for Forensic Sciences Advisory Board, University of Central Florida, 1997 to 2001.
- Trained as an Inspector for the American Society of Crime Laboratory Directors/Laboratory Accreditation Board (ASCLD-LAB), 1998
- Member of Forensic Science Evaluation Team to Ministry of Internal Affairs of Russia, 1997
- Delegate to 1994 International Forensic Science Symposium, Taiwan

- People to People Forensic Science Project delegate to the USSR, 1988.
- Served as a management consultant for Marion County Crime Laboratory, Indianapolis, Indiana performing an audit of the laboratory.
- Served on various ASCLD, MAFS, AAFS committees.

Professional Publication/Presentations:

Kreiser, M.J., Vander Kolk, B.W., "Leasing Analytical Instruments: Advantages, Disadvantages, and Contract Procedures," Journal of Forensic Sciences, 27 (3), July 1982, pages 598 - 621.

Several presentations at regional and national forensic science organizations.

Professional Awards:
- Midwestern Association of Forensic Scientists Distinguished Service Award, 1988
- American Society of Crime Laboratory Directors - The Briggs J. White Award, 1998
- Numerous military awards to include Legion of Merit, Bronze Star and Meritorious Service Medal with two Oak Leaf Clusters.
- Illinois State Police awards to include Meritorious Service Medal and Achievement Awards

Personal

Date of Birth: March 16, 1945, Allegan, Michigan
Marital Status: married, two Children
Hobbies: cycling, walking, reading

References: Available upon request

(Updated April 30, 2015)

Bibliography / Notes / Resources

General Bibliography / Notes / Resources:
- Unless otherwise noted, all Scripture quotations are from THE HOLY BIBLE, NEW INTERNATIONAL VERSION®, NIV® Copyright © 1973, 1978, 1984, 2011 by Biblica, Inc.® Used by permission. All rights reserved worldwide.
- Bruce's writings are assumed to be attributed solely to his creation except in circumstances where he provides annotation for the author of the work.

"Who was Bruce VanderKolk?" Bibliography / Notes / Resources:
- This section could take many pages to list all of the accomplishments that Bruce gathered while on the earth. But doing so probably would have embarrassed him so this section has been left intentionally vague. Besides, while important to his family and friends, it would be less than meaningful to the average reader. If you are interested in learning more about Bruce and his accomplishments, there is always the option to perform an Internet search.
- The link between Agent Orange and adverse health affects on those serving in Vietnam is well established and common knowledge. As of the writing of this book, the U.S. Department of Veteran's Affairs has a dedicated web page specifically devoted to Agent Orange (https://www.va.gov/disability/eligibility/ hazardous-materials-exposure/agent-orange/).
- What is not common knowledge is that Bruce was deemed eligible for disability consideration by the VA as a result of his exposure of Agent Orange while in Vietnam. As a family we believe that Bruce would have approved the release of this information to the general public.
- The "Personal Testimony" section was written by Bruce, with the calling out from the specific version of the Bible referenced in

157

the document. Although it was written in the midst of his fight with bladder cancer, the message is relevant for this portion of his life as well. There is no doubt whether this was written by Bruce for himself or that it was written for others. Bruce wrote it to provide strength and encouragement to others going through similar battles and struggles.

"How then to Thrive?" Bibliography / Notes / Resources:
- This section is written entirely by the author.
- Bruce didn't use the word "thrive" in his journal nor in his writing. The intent of this section is to bring definition to Bruce's thought process when he was documenting his struggles. What did he want to accomplish? Was it for him? It clearly was for others. But why? What was the driving factor for this intensely private man to share his struggles with others? It is easy to determine that he wanted to help others as they navigated through life's struggles. He wanted to help them thrive.
- The definitions of words are pulled from Webster's online dictionary (www.merriam-webster.com)

"Bruce's Journey: Diagnosis" Bibliography / Notes / Resources:
- This section begins to bring forth technical (and sometimes complicated) medical discussions as Bruce absorbs the messages from his doctors. This is important for Bruce because his analytical mind would want to create as precise of a battle plan as possible. The specific detail will only be helpful to those readers going through a similar struggle, but is included to highlight Bruce's thought process.
- In addition to research of written articles and other pages online, Bruce would watch videos of the surgery online before he had the surgery. He wanted to know what was going to be done to his body and what he should expect after the surgery.
- July 27, 2009: Bruce spent much time researching prostate cancer. He found the content material on the Mayo Clinic website very useful and informative. The website is: www.mayoclinic.org.
- "Hallelujah for Every Broken Heart": There are a few song lyrics mentioned in this book, most are a part of David Crowder's

album, "Milk and Honey". Mr. Crowder is on record that the intent of the album is to capture the transition of the Israelites from the desert to the promised land, the land of "milk and honey." (https://www.klove.com/music/blog/behind-the-music/k-love-cover-story-crowders-new-album-milk-and-honey-points-toward-the-post-pandemic-promised-land-2316). I wish this album had been available to Dad as he went through his struggles. There is no doubt in my mind that it would have provided encouragement to him.

- October 30, 2009: Bruce learned a great deal about getting through prostate cancer from the book "How We Survived Prostate Cancer" by Victoria Hallerman. He provides credit to Hallerman in the appropriate journal entry. This book was a great tool for Bruce. The references in this section are included directly from Bruce's writings; the author bears no responsibility to the content or whether a website domain address has been changed.

- October 30, 2009: Hallerman created a list of websites that would be helpful to the caregiver. This list can be found in her book.

- November 2, 2009: Bruce also learned a great deal from reading "Guide to Surviving Prostate Cancer" by Dr. Patrick Walsh. He found the nutrition advice as noted in the November 2, 2009 journal entry especially helpful. Of course he didn't necessarily follow the advice strictly (or even loosely), but Bruce liked this book the most out of the books he found.

- In the Connecting section, the source for the definition of the word "devastating" was www.merriam-webster.com.

- November 19, 2009: Another reference to Dr. Patrick Walsh's book: "A Guide to Surviving Prostate Cancer".

"Bruce's Journey: Treatment" Bibliography / Notes / Resources:
- PSA: The cancer stats for prostate were pulled from the following American Cancer Society webpage on 10/20/21: https://www.cancer.org/cancer/prostate-cancer/about/key-statistics.html

- December 31, 2009: Bruce read the "Ragamuffin Gospel" written by Brennan Manning and it really spoke to him as he was coming to grips with living with a disease, that left untreated, would ultimately take his life. This book was instrumental during Bruce's struggle because it provided the framework of the relationship between life and death on this earth and how to live in the Hope of the next life. His closing statement in this entry says it all: *"My question now is what I can do with God's help to make this a positive experience for me and others"*. The journal entry provides credit to the author, as well as the specific pages in the book that were most insightful to Bruce. The book can be found in bookstores and online.

- In the "Abba, Father" writing, Bruce references a song sung during a special music portion of a church service. The song was titled "Abba, Father" by Hillsong Worship.

"Bruce's Journey: Beyond Cancer" Bibliography / Notes / Resources:

- As Bruce's medical issues surge and require visits with numerous doctors, this section became messy to keep doctors' names in confidence. This also applies to the various medical facilities that Bruce visited.
- The May 22, 2012 journal entry provides a quote from Job 14:1-2 from the NIV translation.
- June 7, 2012: Much of the technical information about the parathyroid in this entry was based on Bruce's online research, specifically the following website: http://www.parathyroid.com/parathyroid.htm.

"Bruce's Journey: A Series of Events" Bibliography / Notes / Resources:

- Some of the journal entries required thought as to whether to include them or not, specifically the issues with the thyroid not being removed during Bruce's initial surgery. The decision was made to include the story/entries because there was no malpractice suit nor any non-disclosure settlement. It was important to include the issue because it showed yet another struggle that Bruce went through. Not only did he face the physical issue of the thyroid not being removed, but he went through mental and emotional issues as well with the frustration of the bad outcome from the first surgery, the investigation into what was said and recorded after the first surgery, and the decision process about whether to pursue legal action. This was a very trying time for Bruce and it is important to share how he navigated through it without losing his focus on his mission, to help others.

"Guide to Thriving" Bibliography / Notes / Resources:
- All Scripture quotations are from THE HOLY BIBLE, NEW INTERNATIONAL VERSION®, NIV® Copyright © 1973, 1978, 1984, 2011 by Biblica, Inc.® Used by permission. All rights reserved worldwide.

"Appendices" Bibliography / Notes / Resources:
- Bruce continued to update his "CV" (ie: Resume) even after he retired.

www.ingramcontent.com/pod-product-compliance
Lightning Source LLC
Chambersburg PA
CBHW051524120626
46551CB00012B/1072